WITHDRAWN

THE ZEN DOCTRINE OF NO-MIND

RIDER

THE ZEN DOCTRINE
OF NO-MIND

The Significance of the Sūtra of
Hui-neng (Wei-lang)

DAISETZ TEITARO SUZUKI, D.Litt
Late Professor of Buddhist Philosophy
in the Otani University, Kyoto

Edited by
CHRISTMAS HUMPHREYS
Late President of the Buddhist Society, London

RIDER
LONDON SYDNEY AUCKLAND JOHANNESBURG

First published 1949, second edition 1969

Reissued as a Rider Pocket Edition 1983
Reprinted 1986, 1990
Rider & Company, an imprint of Century Hutchinson Limited,
20 Vauxhall Bridge Road, London SW1V 2SA

Century Hutchinson Publishing Group (Australia) Pty Ltd
20 Alfred Street, Milsons Point, Sydney, NSW 2061,
Australia

Century Hutchinson Group (NZ) Ltd
32-34 View Road, PO Box 40-086, Glenfield, Auckland 10,
New Zealand

Century Hutchinson Group (SA) Pty Ltd.
PO Box 337, Bergvlei 2012, South Africa

British Library Cataloguing in Publication Data

Suzuki, Daisetz Teitaro
The Zen doctrine of no-mind
1. Zen Buddhism
I. Title   II. Humphreys, Christmas
294.3′927   BQ 9265.4

Printed and bound in Great Britain by
The Guernsey Press Co. Ltd,
Guernsey, Channel Islands.

This American Edition by
Samuel Weiser, Inc.
York Beach, ME 03910
ISBN 0-87728-182-3

EDITOR'S NOTE

THE LATE DAISETZ TEITARO SUZUKI, Professor of Buddhist Philosophy in the Otani University, Kyoto, was born in 1870 and died in 1966. He was probably the greatest living authority of Buddhist philosophy, and was the greatest authority on Zen Buddhism. His major works in English on the subject of Buddhism numbered twenty or more, and of his works in Japanese as yet unknown to the West there are at least eighteen. He was, moreover, as a chronological bibliography of books on Zen in English clearly shows, the pioneer teacher of the subject outside Japan, for excepting Kaiten Nukariya's *Religion of the Samurai* (Luzac and Co., 1913) nothing was known of Zen as a living experience, save to the readers of *The Eastern Buddhist* (1921–1939), until the publication of his *Essays in Zen Buddhism* in 1927.

Dr. Suzuki wrote with authority. Not only had he studied original works in Sanskrit, Pali, Chinese and Japanese, but he had an up-to-date knowledge of Western thought in German and French as well as in the English which he spoke and wrote so fluently. He was, moreover, more than a scholar; he was a Buddhist. Though not a priest of any Buddhist sect, he was honoured in every temple in Japan, for his knowledge of spiritual things, as all who sat at his feet bear witness, was direct and profound. When he spoke of the higher stages of consciousness he spoke as a man who dwelt therein, and the impression he made on those who entered the fringes of his mind was that of a man who sought for the intellectual symbols wherewith to describe a state of awareness which lies indeed 'beyond the intellect'.

To those unable to sit at the feet of the Master his writings

5

must be a substitute. To this end an attempt was made soon after the last war to collect the works of Dr. Suzuki into one collected edition published by Rider & Co., and some eight volumes were so produced.

Of Zen itself I need say nothing here, but the increasing sale of books on the subject, such as R. H. Blyth's *Zen in English Literature,* my own *Zen Buddhism,* Alan Watts' *Way of Zen* and Herrigel's *Zen in the Art of Archery,* together with the series of original translations from Zen classics published by the Buddhist Society, such as *The Sutra of Hui Neng* and *The Zen Teachings of Huang Po,* prove that the interest of the West is still rising. Zen, however, is a subject extremely easy to misunderstand, and it is therefore important that the words of a qualified writer, teaching out of the awareness bred of his own enlightenment, should come readily to hand.

This volume, dedicated largely to the teaching of Hui Neng, covers the whole purpose and technique of Zen training, and in the view of many goes further into the deeps of Zen than any other work of modern times.

CHRISTMAS HUMPHREYS
Late President of the Buddhist Society, London

THE ZEN DOCTRINE
OF NO-MIND

THERE are two significant names in the early history of Zen Buddhism in China. One of them is naturally Bodhi-Dharma[1] as the founder of Zen, and the other is Hui-neng (Wei-lang in the Southern dialect, Yeno in Japanese, 638-713), who determined the course of Zen thought as originated by Bodhi-Dharma. Without Hui-neng and his immediate disciples, Zen might never have developed as it did in the early T'ang period of Chinese history. In the eighth century A.D. Hui-neng's work, known as the Platform Sermons of the Sixth Patriarch (*Lu-tso T'an-ching*, or *Rokuso Dangyo* in Japanese), thus occupied a very important position in Zen, and the vicissitudes of fate which it has suffered are remarkable. It was through this work that Bodhi-Dharma's office as the first proclaimer of Zen thought in China came to be properly defined. It was also through this work that the outline of Zen thought was delineated for his followers as the pattern for their spiritual discipline. By Hui-neng modern Zen Yogins are linked to Bodhi-Dharma, and from him we may date the birth of Chinese Zen as distinct from its Indian form. When we declare the *T'an-ching* to be a work of great consequence it is in this double sense. The roots of its thought extend through Bodhi-Dharma to the enlightenment of the Buddha himself, while its branches spread all over the Far East, where Zen has found its most fruitful soil. It is over a thousand years since Hui-neng's proclamation about Zen was first made, and although since then it has

[1] Various authorities give different dates for his coming to China from Southern India, ranging from A.D. 486 to 527. But following Kaisu (Ch'i-sung) of the Sung dynasty, author of *An Essay on the Orthodox Transmission of the Dharma*, I regard his coming as taking place in 520 and his death in 528.

passed through various stages of development, its essential spirit remains that of the *T'an-ching*. For this reason, if we want to follow the history of Zen thought, we must study the work of Hui-neng, the Sixth Patriarch, in its dual relationship, on the one hand to Bodhi-Dharma and his successors, Hui-Ke, Seng-Tsan, Tao-hsin and Hung-jen, and on the other to Hui-neng himself and his personal disciples and contemporaries.

That the *T'an-ching* was considered by Hui-neng's followers to contain the essential teaching of the Master, and was transmitted among his disciples as a spiritual legacy whose possessor alone could be regarded as a member of the orthodox School of Hui-neng, is shown by the following passage in the *T'an-ching*:

'The great Master stayed at Ts'ao-chi San, and his spiritual influence spread for more than forty years over the two neighbouring provinces of Shao and Kuang. His disciples, including monks and laymen, numbered over three or even five thousand, indeed more than one could reckon. As regards the essence of his teaching, the *T'an-ching* is transmitted as an authoritative pledge, and those who have it not are considered as having no commission [that is, as not having fully understood the teaching of Hui-neng]. When a commission takes place from Master to disciple the place, date and name are to be specified. When there is no handing over of the *T'an-ching* no one can claim to be a disciple of the Southern School. Those who have no *T'an-ching* committed to their care have no essential understanding of the doctrine of the "sudden awakening", even though they preach it. For they are sure to be sooner or later involved in a dispute, and those who have the Dharma should devote themselves only to its practice. Disputes arise from the desire for conquest, and these are not in accordance with the Way.' (The Suzuki and Koda edition of the Tung-huang MS., par. 38.)

Passages of a similar import, though not so explicit, also

occur in the first paragraph of the *T'an-ching*, as in the 47th and 57th. These repetitions are sufficient to prove that this work, as containing the gist of the Sermons given by Hui-neng, was highly prized by his disciples, and the Tun-huang MS. (par. 55) and the Koshoji edition (par. 56) record the names of the persons through whom the Sermons were transmitted. The popular edition, which is generally based on the Yüan edition of the thirteenth century, does not contain the passages relating to the transmission, and the reason for the omission will be discussed later.

There is no doubt that Hui-neng's Sermons created a great sensation among the Buddhists of his day, perhaps because no Buddhist master before him had made such a direct appeal to the masses. The study of Buddhism until then had been more or less restricted to the learned classes, and whatever discourses were given by the masters were based on the orthodox texts. They were scholarly discussions in the nature of a commentary which demanded much erudition and analytical intellection. They did not necessarily reflect facts of personal religious life and experience, but dealt chiefly with concepts and diagrams. Hui-neng's Sermons, on the other hand, expressed his own spiritual intuitions, and were consequently full of vitality, while the language used was fresh and original. This was one reason at least for the unprecedented way in which they were received by the public as well as by professional scholars. This was also the reason why Hui-neng was made in the beginning of the *T'an-ching* to narrate his own story at great length, for if he were just an ordinary scholar-monk belonging to the Buddhist hierarchy of his day there would be no necessity for him, or rather for his immediate followers, to explain himself. That the followers made so much of the illiteracy of their Master had no doubt a great deal to do with his uniqueness of character and career.

The story of his life, which opens the *T'an-ching*, is told in the form of an autobiography, but is more likely to be the work of the compiler or compilers of the work itself. Certainly the passage in which Hui-neng is depicted in such loud and glaring contrast to Shen-hsiu, who came to be regarded as his rival, cannot come from Hui-neng's own mouth. The rivalry between the two men developed after the death of their master, Hung-jen; that is, only when each began to propagate the Zen teaching according to the light of his own realization. It is even uncertain whether the two men were under their common master at the same time. Shen-hsiu was over a hundred when he died in 706, and at that time Hui-neng was only 69. There was thus at least thirty years' difference between them, and according to *The Life of Hui-neng*, brought over to Japan by Saicho in 803, Hui-neng was 34, when he came to Hung-jen to study under him. If Shen-hsiu were still with the master, he must have been between 64 and 70, and it said that Shen-hsiu stayed with Hung-jen for six years, and again that Hung-jen passed away soon after Hui-neng left him. It is just possible that Shen-hsiu's sixth year with Hung-jen was coincidental with the appearance of Hui-neng at the Yellow Plum Monastery. But if Shen-hsiu was so behind Hui-neng in his attainment, even after six years' study and self-training, and if his master died soon after Hui-neng's leaving the Brotherhood, when could Shen-hsiu have completed his course of Zen discipline? According to the documents relating to him, he was evidently one of the most accomplished masters of Zen under Hung-jen, and also of his time. The story of Shen-hsiu as related in the *T'an-ching* must therefore be a fiction created by its compilers after the death of Hui-neng himself, for the rivalry, so called, between the two masters was really the rivalry between their respective followers, who carried it on at the expense of their respective masters.

In the story which opens the *T'an-ching*, Hui-neng tells where he was born, and how ignorant he was of all the classical literature of China. He then proceeds to tell how he became interested in Buddhism by listening to the reading of the Vajracchedikā Sūtra, which he himself did not know how to read. When he went up to Huang-mei Shan (the Yellow Plum Mountain) to study Zen under Hung-jen, the Fifth Patriarch, he was not an ordained monk belonging to the Brotherhood, but an ordinary layman, and he asked to be allowed to work in the granary as a labourer attached to the institution. While thus engaged he was evidently not allowed to mingle with the monks, and knew nothing about things going on in other parts of the monastery.

There is, however, at least one statement in the *T'an-ching* and in Hui-neng's biography[1] which points to occasional interviews between Hui-neng and his master, Hung-jen. When Hung-jen announced that any one of his disciples who could compose a satisfactory *gāthā* expressing his views on Zen would succeed him as Sixth Patriarch, Hui-neng was not told about it; he was to all intents and purposes a mere labourer attached to the monastery. But Hung-jen must have had some knowledge of the spiritual attainment of Hui-neng, and must have expected that some day, somehow, his accouncement would reach him.

Hui-neng could not even write his own composition, and had to ask someone to write it for him. There are frequent references in the *T'an-ching* to his inability to read the Sūtras, although he understood the meaning when they were read to him. The rivalry between Hui-neng and Shen-hsiu, strongly but one-sidedly brought out in all the records now available (except in Saicho's biography above mentioned, which makes no reference to Shen-hsiu), was no doubt emphasized by the immediate disciples of

[1] This biography, known as the Ts'ao-chi Yueh Chuan, was evidently compiled soon after the passing of Hui-neng, and was brought to Japan by Saicho, the founder of the Japanese Tendai (T'ien-tai) Sect, in 803, when he returned from China, where he had been studying Buddhism. It is the most reliable historical document relating to Hui-neng.

Hui-neng who, however, proved to be the winners in the struggle. The main reason for this was that Hui-neng's 'Southern' Zen was more in accord with the spirit of Mahāyāna Buddhism, and with Chinese psychology, than the 'Northern' School of Shen-hsiu. Erudition always tends to abstraction and conceptualism, obscuring the light of intuition, which is principally needed in the religious life. Shen-hsiu, in spite of the records made of him by Hui-neng's followers, was certainly worthy of carrying the robe and bowl of his master, but his presentation of Buddhism naturally required a far more elaborate and learned methodology than that of Hui-neng, and the spirit of Zen abhors all forms of intellectualism. Hui-neng's alleged illiteracy more boldly brings out the truth and force of his Buddhist intuitions, and glaringly sets off the conceptualism of Shen-hsiu's teaching. And it is a well-established fact that the Chinese mind prefers to deal with concrete realities and actual experiences. As the first great native expounder of Zen, Hui-neng exactly fulfilled a need.

But was he so illiterate? True, he was not a learned scholar, but I do not think of him as so illiterate as he is made out to be in the *T'an-ching*. To accentuate the contrast between him and Shen-hsiu it was more dramatic to picture him as incapable of understanding literature, even as Christ when arguing with the erudite, grey-haired scribes whose discourse had no authority. Yet it is a fact that the religious genius does not need so much help from knowledge and intellection as from the richness of the inner life.

The *T'an-ching* contains allusions to several Sūtras, showing that the author was not altogether an ignoramus, but though, being a Buddhist, he naturally resorted to Buddhist terminology, he is entirely free from pedantic scholasticism. Compared with other Buddhist teachers of his age he is direct, and goes to the heart of his teaching without circumlocution. This simplicity must have greatly impressed his audience, especially those who were spiritually inclined and yet endowed with a certain kind of intellectuality. It was they who took notes of his Sermons, and treasured them as precious documents containing deeply religious intuitions.

The original idea of Hui-neng was, of course, to do away with verbalism and literature, because Mind can only be comprehended by mind directly and without a medium. But human nature is everywhere the same, and even Zen followers have their weaknesses, one of which is to have given too much importance to the documentary remains of the Master. The *T'an-ching* thus came to be regarded as the symbol of truth in which Zen is securely embedded, and it may be said that where the *T'an-ching* is treasured too highly, there the spirit of Zen is beginning to decline. It is perhaps because of this that the book ceased to be transmitted from Master to disciple as a kind of insignia certifying the latter's attainment of the truth of Zen. And it is perhaps for this reason that the passages above quoted relating to the transmission were struck out from the current edition of the *T'an-ching*, which thereafter came to be looked on simply as a work teaching the doctrine of Zen as propagated by Hui-neng.

Whatever the reason, the meaning of Hui-neng's appearance in the early history of Zen Buddhism was highly significant, and the *T'an-ching* deserves to be considered a monumental work, as having determined the course of Buddhist thought in China for many centuries to come.

Before we proceed to expound Hui-neng's views on Buddhism, let us present those of Shen-hsiu, which are always presented in contrast to the former because the rivalry between the two leaders helped to define the nature of Zen more clearly than before. Hung-jen was a great Zen Master, and had many capable followers, more than a dozen of whose names are preserved in history. But Hui-neng and Shen-hsiu stood far above the rest, and it was under them that Zen came to be divided into two schools, the Southern and Northern. When we know, therefore, what was taught by Shen-hsiu, the leader of the Northern School, it will be easier to understand Hui-neng, with whom we are here principally concerned.

Unfortunately, however, we are not in possession of much of the teaching of Shen-hsiu, for the fact that this School failed to prosper against its competitor led to the disappearance of its literature. What we do know of it comes from two sources: first, the documents belonging to the Southern School, such as the *T'an-ching* and Tsung-mi's writings, and secondly, two Tun-huang MSS. which I found in the Bibliothèque Nationale in Paris. One of these two writings of the Northern School is incomplete and the other is imperfect in meaning, and Shen-hsiu did not write either himself. As in the *T'an-ching*, the MS. is a kind of notes taken by his disciples of the Master's lectures.

The MS. is entitled 'The Teaching of the Five Means by the Northern School'. Here the word 'means' or method, *upāya* in Sanskrit, is not apparently used in any special sense, and the five means are five heads of reference to the Mahāyāna Sūtras as to the teaching in the Northern School. This teaching is (1) Buddhahood is enlightenment, and enlightenment consists is not awakening the mind. (2) When the mind is kept immovable the senses are quietened, and in this state the gate of supreme knowledge opens. (3) This opening of supreme knowledge leads to a mystical emancipation of mind and body. This, however, does not mean the absolute quietism of the Nirvāṇa of the Hīnayānists, for the supreme knowledge attained by Bodhisattvas involves unattached activity of the senses. (4) This unattached activity means being free from the dualism of mind and body, wherein the true character of things is grasped. (5) Finally, there is the path of Oneness, leading to a world of Suchness which knows no obstructions, no differences. This is Enlightenment.

It is interesting to compare this with the comment of Tsung-mi of the Southern School. As he writes in his *Diagram of Patriarchal Succession of the Zen Teaching*: 'The Northern School teaches that all beings are originally endowed with Enlightenment, just as it is the nature of a mirror to illuminate. When the passions veil the mirror it is invisible, as though obscured with dust. If, according to the instructions of the Master, erroneous thoughts are subdued and annihilated, they cease to rise. Then the mind is enlightened as to its own nature, leaving nothing unknown. It is like brushing the mirror. When there is no more dust the mirror shines out, leaving nothing unillumined.' Therefore Shen-hsiu, the great Master and leader of this School, writes, in his *gāthā* presented to the Fifth Patriarch:

> This body is the Bodhi-tree.
> The mind is like a mirror bright;
> Take heed to keep it always clean
> And let not dust collect upon it.

Further on, Tsung-mi illustrates the position of Shen-hsiu by means of a crystal ball. The mind, he says, is like a crystal ball with no colour of its own. It is pure and perfect as it is. But as soon as it confronts the outside world it takes on all colours and forms of differentiation. This differentiation is in the outside world, and the mind, left to itself, shows no change of any character. Now suppose the ball to be placed against something altogether contrary to itself, and so become a dark-coloured ball. However pure it may have been before, it is now a dark-coloured ball, and this colour is seen as belonging from the first to the nature of the ball. When shown thus to ignorant people they will at once conclude that the ball is foul, and will not be easily convinced of its essential purity. Even those who knew it when pure will now pronounce it soiled by seeing it so, and will endeavour to polish it, to enable it to regain what it has lost. These polishers, according to Tsung-mi, are followers of the Northern School, imagining that the crystal ball in its purity is to be discovered under the darkened state in which they found it.

This dust-wiping attitude of Shen-hsiu and his followers inevitably leads to the quietistic method of meditation, and it was indeed the method which they recommended. They taught the entering into a Samādhi by means of concentration, and the purifying of the mind by making it dwell on one thought. They further taught that by the awakening of thoughts an objective world was illumined, and that when they were folded up an inner world was perceived.

Shen-hsiu, like other Zen masters, recognizes that the Mind exists, and that this is to be sought within one's own individual mind, which is endowed with all the Buddha virtues. That this fact is not realized is due to our habitual running after outside objects which darken the light of the inner mind. Instead of flying away from one's own father, advises Shen-hsiu, one should look within by the practice of tranquillization. This is all very well so far as it goes, but Shen-hsiu lacks metaphysical penetration, and his method suffers from this deficiency. It is what is generally designated as 'artificial' or 'doing something' (*yu-tso*), and not as 'doing nothing' (*wu-tso*), or as 'being in itself' (*tzu-hsing*).

The following record in the *T'an-ching* will be illuminating when seen in the light of the above statement.[1]

40. 'Shen-hsiu, observing people making remarks about Hui-neng's direct and quick method of pointing at the truth, called in one of his own disciples named Chi-ch'eng, and said: "You have a very intelligent mind, full of wisdom. Go for my sake to Ts'ao-ch'i Shan, and when you get to Hui-neng pay him respect and just listen to him. Don't let him know that you have come from me. As soon

[1] The Tun-huang MS., §§ 40 and 41. The Koshoji copy, §§ 42 and 43.

as you get the meaning of what you listen to, keep it in
mind and come back to me, and tell me all about him. I will
then see whether his understanding is the quick one, or
mine."

'Obeying his master's orders with a joyful heart, Chi-
ch'eng reached Ts'ao-ch'i Shan after about a half-month's
journey. He paid due respect to Hui-neng, and listened to
him without letting him know whence he came. While
listening, Chi-ch'eng's mind at once grasped the purport
of Hui-neng's teaching. He knew what his original Mind is.
He stood up and made bows, saying: "I come from the
Yu-ch'uan monastery, but under my Master, Hsiu, I have
not been able to come to the realization. Now, listening to
your Sermon, I have at once come to the knowledge of the
original Mind. Be merciful, O Master, and teach me further
about it."

'Hui-neng, the great Master, said: "If you come from
there, you are a spy."

'Chi-ch'eng said: "When I did not declare myself, I was
(a spy); but after my declaration I am not."

'The Sixth Patriarch said: "So it is also with the statement that the passions (*kleśa*) are no other than enlightenment (*bodhi*)." '

41. 'The great Master said to Chi-ch'eng: "I hear that
your Master only instructs people in the triple discipline of
Precepts (*śīla*), Meditation (*dhyāna*), and Transcendental
Knowledge (*prajñā*). Tell me how your Master does this."

'Chi-ch'eng said: "The Master, Hsiu, teaches the Precepts, Meditation, and Knowledge in this way: Not to do
evil is the precept; to do all that is good is knowledge;
to purify one's own mind is meditation. This is his view of
the triple discipline, and his teaching is in accord with this.
What is your view, O Master?"

'Hui-neng replied: "This is a wonderful view, but mine is
different."

'Chi-ch'eng asked: "How different?"

'Hui-neng replied: "There is a slow view, and there is a quick view."

'Chi-ch'eng begged the Master to explain *his* view of the Precept, Meditation, and Knowledge.

'The great Master said: "Listen to my teaching, then. According to my view, the Mind as it is in itself is free from ills—this is the Precept of Self-being. The Mind as it is in itself is free from disturbances—this is the Meditation of Self-being. The Mind as it is in itself is free from follies— this is the Knowledge of Self-being."

'Hui-neng, the great Master, continued: "The Triple Discipline as taught by your Master is meant for people of inferior endowments, whereas my teaching of the Triple Discipline is for superior people. When Self-being is understood, there is no further use in establishing the Triple Discipline."

'Chi-ch'eng said: "Pray tell me about the meaning of this 'no further use'."

'The great Master said: "[The Mind as] Self-being is free from ills, disturbances and follies, and every thought is thus of transcendental knowledge; and within the reach of this illuminating light there are no forms to be recognized as such. Being so, there is no use in establishing anything. One is awakened to this Self-being abruptly, and there is no gradual realization in it. This is the reason for no-establishment."

'Chi-ch'eng made bows, and never left Ts'ao-ch'i Shan. He became a disciple of the great Master and attended him always.'

From this contrast between Shen-hsiu and Hui-neng we can understand why Shen-hsiu's view of the Triple Discipline is designated by Shen-hui, one of the great disciples of Hui-neng, as belonging to the type of 'doing something', while that of Hui-neng is the type of Self-being which is characterized as empty, serene and illuminating. Shen-hui gives a third type, called 'doing nothing', by which the Triple Discipline is understood in this way: 'When erroneous thoughts do not rise, this is Precept; when erroneous thoughts are no more, this is Meditation; and when the non-existence of erroneous thoughts is perceived, this is Transcendental Knowledge. The 'nothing doing' type and the 'self-being' type are the same; the one states negatively what the other states positively.

Besides these, Shen-hsiu is stated to have expressed his views on the following five subjects, depending on the *Awakening of Faith in the Mahāyāna, the Saddharma-puṇḍarīka, the Vimalakīrti Sūtra, the Shiyaku-kyo,* and *the Avataṁsaka-Sūtra.* The five subjects are: (1) the Buddha-body which means perfect enlightenment expressing itself as the Dharmakāya of the Tathāgata; (2) the intuitive knowledge belonging to the Buddha, which is kept thoroughly defiled by the six senses; (3) emancipation beyond intellectual measures, which belongs to the Bodhisattva; (4) the true nature of all things as remaining serene and undisturbed; and (5) the absolutely unimpeded passageway opened to the course of enlightenment which is attained by penetrating into the truth of non-differentiation.

These views held by Shen-hsiu are interesting enough in themselves, but as they do not concern us here we shall not go into a detailed exposition. We will now proceed to Hui-neng.

W HAT distinguishes Hui-neng most conspicuously and characteristically from his predecessors as well as from his contemporaries is his doctrine of 'hon-rai mu-ichi-motsu' (*pen-lai wu-i-wu*). This is one of the lines declared against Shen-hsiu's *gāthā* to which reference has already been made. The whole *gāthā* by Hui-neng runs thus:

> There is no Bodhi-tree,
> Nor stand of mirror bright.
> Since all is void,
> Where can the dust alight?

'From the first not a thing is'—this was the first proclamation made by Hui-neng. It is a bomb thrown into the camp of Shen-hsiu and his predecessors. By it Hui-neng's Zen came to be sharply outlined against the background of the dust-brushing type of Zen meditation. Shen-hsiu was not exactly wrong in his view, for there is reason to suppose that Shen-hsiu's own teacher, Hung-jen, the Fifth Patriarch, who was also Hui-neng's teacher, had a similar view, though this was not so explicitly stated as Shen-hsiu's. In fact, Hung-jen's teaching could be construed in either way, in that of Shen-hsiu or in that of Hui-neng. Hung-jen was a great master of Zen and from him grew up many strong personalities who became great spiritual leaders of the time. Of them Shen-hsiu and Hui-neng were the most distinguished in many ways, and the camp came to be divided between them. Shen-hsiu interpreted Hung-jen in his own light, and Hui-neng in his, and, as already explained, the latter as time went on proved to be the winner as being in better accord with the thought and psychology of the Chinese people.

In all likelihood there was in Hung-jen's teaching itself something which tended to that of Shen-hsiu, for Hung-jen seems to have instructed his pupils to 'keep their guard on the Mind' all the time. He, of course, being a follower of Bodhi-Dharma, believed in the Mind from which this universe with all its multiplicities issues, but which in itself is simple, undefiled, and illuminating as the sun behind the clouds. 'To keep one's guard on this original Mind' means to keep it clear from the beclouding mists of individualization, so that its pure light may be retained intact and ever illuminating. But in this view the conception of the Mind and of its relation to the world of multiplicities is not clearly defined, and there is every probability of getting these concepts confused.

If the Mind is originally pure and undefiled, why is it necessary to brush off its dust, which comes from nowhere? Is not this dust-wiping, which is the same thing as 'keeping one's guard', an unwarranted process on the part of the Zen Yogin? The wiping is indeed an altogether unnecessary contrivance. If from the Mind arises this world, why not let the latter rise as it pleases? To try to stop its rising by keeping one's guard on the Mind—is not this interfering with the mind? The most logical and most natural thing to do in relation to the Mind would be to let it go on with its creating and illuminating.

Hung-jen's teaching of guarding the Mind may mean to guard on the part of the Yogin his own individual mind from getting in the way of the original Mind. But at the same time there is the danger of the Yogin's acting exactly contrary to the doctrine of non-interference. This is a delicate point, and the masters have to be quite definite about it—not only in concepts but in the practical methods of training. The master himself may have a well-defined idea of what he desires to accomplish in the pupil's mind, but the latter too frequently fails to move in unison with the master. For this reason, methods must vary not only with persons but with ages. And again, for this reason differences are more vehemently asserted among the disciples than between two masters advocating different methods.

Shen-hsiu was perhaps more inclined to teach the self-guarding or dust-wiping process than the letting-alone process. This latter, however, has in its turn deep pitfalls into which its devotees may fall. For it is fundamentally the outcome of the doctrine of emptiness or nothingness; that is, the idea that 'from the first not a thing is'.

When Hui-neng declared, 'From the first not a thing is', the keynote of his Zen thought was struck, and from it we recognize the extent of difference there is between him and his predecessors and contemporaries. This keynote was never so clearly struck before. When the Masters who followed him pointed to the presence of the Mind in each individual mind and also to its absolute purity, this idea of presence and purity was understood somehow to suggest the existence of an individual body, however ethereal and transparent it may be conceived. And the result was to dig out this body from the heap of obscuring materials. On the other hand, Hui-neng's concept of nothingness (*wu-i-wu*) may push one down into a bottomless abyss, which will no doubt create a feeling of utter forlornness. The philosophy of Prajñāpāramitā, which is also that of Hui-neng, generally has this effect. To understand it a man requires a deep religious intellectual insight into the truth of Śūnyatā. When Hui-neng is said to have had an awakening by listening to the *Vajracchedikā Sūtra* (Diamond Sūtra) which belongs to the Prajñāpāramitā group of the Mahāyāna texts, we know at once where he has his foothold.

The dominant idea prevailing up to the time of Hui-neng was that the Buddha-nature with which all beings are endowed is thoroughly pure and undefiled as to its self-being. The business of the Yogin is therefore to bring out his self-nature, which is the Buddha-nature, in its original purity. But, as I said before, in practice this is apt to lead the Yogin to the conception of something separate which retains its purity behind all the confusing darkness enveloping his individual mind. His meditation may end in clearing up the mirror of consciousness in which he expects to see the image of his original pure self-being reflected. This may be called static meditation. But serenely reflecting or contemplating on the purity of the Mind has a suicidal effect on life, and Hui-neng vehemently protested against this type of meditation.

In the *T'an-ching*, and other Zen works after it, we often come across the term '*K'an-ching*', meaning 'to keep an eye on Purity', and this practice is condemned. 'To keep an eye on purity' is no other than a quietistic contemplation of one's self-nature or self-being. When the concept of 'original purity' issues in this kind of meditation, it goes against the true understanding of Zen. Shen-hsiu's teaching was evidently strongly coloured with quietism or the reflection type. So, when Hui-neng proclaimed, 'From the first not a thing is,' the statement was quite original with him, though ultimately it goes back to the *Prajñāpāramitā*. It really revolutionized the Zen practice of meditation, establishing what is really Buddhist and at the same time preserving the genuine spirit of Bodhi-Dharma.

Hui-neng and his followers now came to use the new term *chien-hsing* instead of the old *k'an-ching*. *Chien-hsing* means 'to look into the nature [of the Mind]'. *K'an* and *chien* both relate to the sense of sight, but the character *k'an*, which consists of a hand and an eye, is to watch an object as independent of the spectator; the seen and the seeing are two separate entities. *Chien*, composed of an eye alone on two outstretched legs, signifies the pure act of seeing. When it is coupled with *hsing*, Nature, or Essence, or Mind, it is seeing into the ultimate nature of things, and not watching, as the Samkhya's Purusha watches the dancing of Prakrit. The seeing is not reflecting on an object as if the seer had nothing to do with it. The seeing, on the contrary, brings the seer and the object seen together, not in mere identification but the becoming conscious of itself, or rather of its working. The seeing is an active deed, involving the dynamic conception of self-being; that is, of the Mind. The distinction made by Hui-neng between *k'an* and *chien* may thus be considered revolutionary in the history of Zen thought.

The utterance, 'From the first not a thing is,' thus effectively destroys the error which attaches itself too frequently to the idea of purity. Purity really means nothingness (*śūnyatā*); it is the negation of all qualities, a state of absolute no-ness, but it somehow tends to create a separate entity outside the 'one who sees'. The fact that *k'an* has been used with it proves that the error has actually been committed. When the idea 'from the first not a thing is' is substituted for 'the self-nature of the Mind is pure and undefiled', all the logical and psychological pedestals which have been given to one are now swept from underneath one's feet and one has nowhere to stand. And this is exactly what is needed for every sincere Buddhist to experience before he can come to the realization of the Mind. The seeing is the result of his having nothing to stand upon. Hui-neng is thus in one way looked upon as the father of Chinese Zen.

It is true that he sometimes uses terms as suggesting the older type of meditation when he speaks about 'cleansing the mind' (*ching-hsin*), 'self-being's originally being pure and undefiled', 'the sun being covered with clouds', etc. Yet his unmistakable condemnation of quietistic meditation rings clearly through his works: 'When you sit quietly with an emptied mind, this is falling into a blank emptiness'; and again:' There are some people with the confused notion that the greatest achievement is to sit quietly with an emptied mind, where not a thought is allowed to be conceived.' Hui-neng thus advises 'neither to cling to the notion of a mind, nor to cling to the notion of purity, nor to cherish the thought of immovability; for these are not our meditation'. 'When you cherish the notion of purity and cling to it, you turn purity into falsehood. . . . Purity has neither form nor shape, and when you claim an achievement by establishing a form to be known as purity, you obstruct your own self-nature, you are purity-bound.' From these passages we can see where Hui-neng wants us to look for final emancipation.

There are as many kinds of binding as there are kinds of clinging. When we cling to purity we thereby make a form of it, and we are purity-bound. For the same reason, when we cling to or abide with emptiness, we are emptiness-bound; when we abide with Dhyāna or tranquillization, we are Dhyāna-bound. However excellent are the merits of these spiritual exercises, they inevitably lead us to a state of bondage in one way or another. In this there is no emancipation. The whole system of Zen discipline may thus be said to be nothing but a series of attempts to set us absolutely free from all forms of bondage. Even when we talk of 'seeing into one's self-nature', this seeing has also a binding effect on us if it is construed as having something in it specifically set up; that is, if the seeing is a specific state of consciousness. For this is the 'binding'.[1]

The Master (Shen-hui) asked Teng: 'What exercise do you recommend in order to see into one's self-nature?'

Teng answered: 'First of all it is necessary to practise meditation by quietly sitting cross-legged. When this exercise is fully mastered, Prajñā (intuitive knowledge) grows out of it, and by virtue of this Prajñā the seeing into one's self-nature is attained.'

Shen-hui inquired: 'When one is engaged in meditation, is this not a specifically contrived exercise?'

'Yes, it is.'

[1] See the *Sayings of Shên-hui*, § 11.

27

'If so, this specific contrivance is an act of limited consciousness, and how could it lead to the seeing of one's self-nature?'

'For this seeing we must exercise ourselves in meditation (*dhyāna*): if not for this exercise, how can one ever see into one's self-nature?'

Shen-hui commented: 'This exercising in meditation owes its function ultimately to an erroneous way of viewing the truth; and as long as this is the case, exercises of such nature would never issue in [true] meditation (*dhyāna*).'

Teng explained: 'What I mean by attaining meditation by exercising oneself in meditation is this. When meditation is attained, an illumination inside and outside comes by itself upon one; and because of this illumination inside and outside, one sees purity; and because of one's mind being pure it is known as seeing into one's nature.'

Shen-hui, however, argued further: 'When the seeing into one's nature is spoken of, we make no reference to this nature as having inside and outside. If you speak of an illumination taking place inside and outside, this is seeing into a mind of error, and how can it be real seeing into one's self-nature? We read in a Sūtra: 'If you are engaged in the mastery of all kinds of Samādhi, that is moving and not sitting in meditation. The mind flows out as it comes in contact with the environment. How can it be called meditation (*dhyāna*)? If this kind of meditation is to be held as genuine, Vimalakīrti would not take Śāriputra to task when the latter claimed to be exercising himself in meditation.'

In these critical questionings Shen-hui exposes the position of Teng and his followers, the advocates of purity; for in them there are still traces of clinging, i.e. setting up a certain state of mind and taking it for ultimate emancipation. So long as the seeing is something to see, it is not the real one; only when the seeing is no-seeing—that is, when the seeing is not a specific act of seeing into a definitely circumscribed state of consciousness—is it the 'seeing into one's self-nature'. Paradoxically stated, when seeing is no-seeing there is real seeing; when hearing is no-hearing there is real hearing. This is the intuition of the Prajñā-pāramitā.

When thus the seeing of self-nature has no reference to a specific state of consciousness, which can be logically or relatively defined as a something, the Zen masters designate it in negative terms and call it 'no-thought' or 'no-mind', *wu-nien* or *wu-hsin*. As it is 'no-thought' or 'no-mind', the seeing is really the seeing. Elsewhere I intend to analyse this concept of 'no-mind' (*wu-hsin*), which is the same thing as 'no-thought' (*wu-nien*), but here let me deal in further detail with the ideas of purity, illumination, and self-nature in order to shed more light on the thought of Hui-neng as one of the greatest Zen masters in the early history of Chinese Zen. To do this, I will take another quotation from *Shên-hui's Sayings*, in which we have these points well illustrated by the most eloquent disciple of Hui-neng.

Chang-yen King asked [Shen-hui]: 'You discourse ordinarily on the subject of Wu-nien ("no-thought" or "no-consciousness"), and make people discipline themselves in it. I wonder if there is a reality corresponding to the notion of Wu-nien, or not?'

Shen-hui answered: 'I would not say that Wu-nien is a reality, nor that it is not.'

'Why?'

'Because if I say it is a reality, it is not in the sense in which people generally speak of reality; if I say it is a non-reality, it is not in the sense in which people generally speak of non-reality. Hence Wu-nien is neither real or unreal.'

'What would you call it then?'

'I would not call it anything.'

'If so, what could it be?'

'No designation whatever is possible. Therefore I say that Wu-nien is beyond the range of wordy discourse. The reason we talk about it at all is because questions are raised concerning it. If no questions are raised about it, there would be no discourse. It is like a bright mirror. If no objects appear before it, nothing is to be seen in it. When you say that you see something in it, it is because something stands against it.'

'When the mirror has nothing to illuminate, the illumination itself loses its meaning, does it not?'

'When I talk about objects presented and their illumination, the fact is that this illumination is something eternal belonging to the nature of the mirror, and has no reference to the presence or absence of objects before it.'

'You say that it has no form, it is beyond the range of wordy discourse, the notion of reality or non-reality is not applicable to it; why then do you talk of illumination? What illumination is it?'

'We talk of illumination because the mirror is bright and its self-nature is illumination. The mind which is present in all things being pure, there is in it the light of Prajñā, which illuminates the entire world-system to its furthest end.'

'This being so, when is it attained?'

'Just see into nothingness (*tan chien wu*).'

'Even if it is nothingness, it is seeing something.'

'Though it is seeing, it is not to be called something.'

'If it is not to be called something, how can there be the seeing?'

'Seeing into nothingness—this is true seeing and eternal seeing.'[1]

---

[1] See the *Sayings of Shên-hui*, § 8.

SEEING INTO ONE'S SELF-NATURE

THE first declaration made by Hui-neng regarding his Zen experience was that 'From the first not a thing is', and then he went on to the 'Seeing into one's self-nature', which self-nature, being 'not a thing', is nothingness. Therefore, 'seeing into one's self-nature' is 'seeing into nothingness', which is the proclamation of Shen-hui. And this seeing is the illuminating of this world of multiplicity by the light of Prajñā. Prajñā thus becomes one of the chief issues discussed in the *T'an-ching*, and this is where the current of Zen thought deviates from the course it had taken from the time of Bodhi-Dharma.

In the beginning of Zen history the centre of interest was in the Buddha-nature or Self-nature, which was inherent in all beings and absolutely pure. This is the teaching of the *Nirvāṇa Sūtra*, and all Zen followers since Bodhi-Dharma are firm believers in it. Hui-neng was, of course, one of them. He was evidently acquainted with this doctrine even before he came to the Fifth Patriarch, Hung-jen, because he insisted on the identity of the Buddha-nature in all beings regardless of the racial or national differences which might be found between himself and his Master. The biography of Hui-neng known as the *Tsao-chi Tai-chi Pieh Tien*, perhaps the earliest literary composition recording his life, has him as listening to the *Nirvāṇa Sūtra* recited by a nun, who was sister to his friend Lin. If Hui-neng were just a student of the *Vajracchedikā*, which we gather from the *T'an-ching*, he could never have talked with Hung-jen as described in the *T'an-ching*. His allusion to the Buddha-nature must no doubt have come from the *Nirvāṇa Sūtra*. With this knowledge, and what he had gained at Hung-jen's, he was able to discourse on the original purity of self-nature and our seeing into this truth as fundamental in the understanding of Zen thought. In Hung-jcn, the teacher of Hui-neng, the idea of Prajñā was not so emphatically brought out as in the disciple. With the latter, the problem of Prajñā, especially in the relation to Dhyāna, is all-absorbing.

Prajñā is primarily one of the three subjects of the Buddhist Triple Discipline, which is Morality (*śīla*), Meditation (*dhyāna*), and Wisdom (*prajñā*). Morality consists in observing all the precepts laid down by the Buddha for the spiritual welfare of his disciples. Meditation is the exercise to train oneself in tranquillization, for as long as the mind is not kept under control by means of meditation it was of no use just to observe mechanically the rules of conduct; in fact, the latter were really meant for spiritual tranquillization. Wisdom or Prajñā is the power to penetrate into the nature of one's being, as well as the truth itself thus intuited. That all these three are needed for a devoted Buddhist goes without saying. But after the Buddha, as time went on, the Triple Discipline was split into three individual items of study. The observers of the rules of morality set down by the Buddha became teachers of the Vināya; the Yogins of meditation were absorbed in various Samādhis, and even acquired something of supernatural faculties, such as clairvoyance, mind-reading, telepathy, knowledge of one's past lives, etc.; and lastly, those who pursued Prajñā became philosophers, dialectricians, or intellectual leaders. This one-sided study of the Triple Discipline made the Buddhists deviate from the proper path of the Buddhist life, especially in Dhyāna (meditation) and Prajñā (wisdom or intuitive knowledge).

This separation of Dhyāna and Prajñā become particularly tragic as time went on, and Prajñā came to be conceived as dynamically seeing into the truth. The separation at its inception had no thought of evil. Yet Dhyāna became the exercise of killing life, of keeping the mind in a state of torpor and making the Yogins socially useless; while

Prajñā, left to itself, lost its profundity, for it was identified with intellectual subtleties which dealt in concepts and their analysis. Then the question arose as to whether or not Dhyāna and Prajñā were two distinct notions, each of which was to be pursued independently of the other. At the time of Hui-neng, the idea of separation was emphasized by Shen-hsiu and his followers, and the result was exercises in purification; that is, in dust-wiping meditation. We can say that Shen-hsiu was the advocate of Dhyāna first and Prajñā second, while Hui-neng almost reversed this, saying that Dhyāna without Prajñā leads to a grave error, but when Prajñā is genuine, Dhyāna comes along with it. According to Hui-neng, Dhyāna is Prajñā and Prajñā is Dhyāna, and when this relation of identity between the two is not grasped there will be no emancipation.

To begin with Dhyāna, Hui-neng's definition is: 'Dhyāna (tso-ch'an) is not to get attached to the mind, is not to get attached to purity, nor is it to concern itself with immovability. . . . What is Dhyāna, then? It is not to be obstructed in all things. Not to have any thought stirred up by the outside conditions of life, good and bad—this is tso (dhyāna). To see inwardly the immovability of one's self-nature—this is ch'an (dhyāna). . . . Outwardly, to be free from the notion of form—this is ch'an. Inwardly, not to be disturbed—this is ting (dhyāna).

'When, outwardly, a man is attached to form, his inner mind is disturbed. But when outwardly he is not attached to form, his mind is not disturbed. His original nature is pure and quiet as it is in itself; only when it recognizes an objective world, and thinks of it as something, is it disturbed. Those who recognize an objective world, and yet find their mind undisturbed, are in true Dhyāna. . . . In the Vimalakīrti it is said that "when a man is instantly awakened, he comes back to his original mind", and in the Bodhi-sattva-śīla, that "My own original self-nature is pure and non-defiled". Thus, O friends, we recognize in each one of

33

the thoughts [we may conceive] the pureness of our original self-nature; to discipline ourselves in this and to practise by ourselves [all its implications]—this is by ourselves to attain Buddha's truth.'

In this we see that Hui-neng's idea of Dhyāna is not at all the traditional one as has been followed and practised by most of his predecessors, especially by those of the Hīna-yāna inclination. His idea is that advocated in the Mahā-yāna, notably by Vimalakīrti, Subhūti, Mañjuśrī and other great Mahāyāna figures.

Hui-neng's attitude towards Dhyāna, meditation, will be more fully illustrated by the following story told of one of his disciples[1]:

'In the eleventh year of Kai-yuan (723 C.E.) there was a Zen master in T'an-chou known as Chih-huang, who once studied under Jen, the great master. Later, he returned to Lu-shan monastery at Chang-sha, where he was devoted to the practice of meditation (tso-chan=dhyāna), and frequently entered into a Samādhi (ting). His reputation reached far and wide.

'At the time there was another Zen master whose name was Tai-yung.[2] He went to Ts'ao-ch'i and studied under the great master for thirty years. The master used to tell him: "You are equipped for missionary work." Yung at last bade farewell to his master and returned north. On the way, passing by Huang's retreat, Yung paid a visit to him and respectfully inquired: "I am told that your reverence frequently enters into a Samādhi. At the time of such entrances, is it supposed that your consciousness still continues, or that you are in a state of unconsciousness? If your consciousness still continues, all sentient beings are endowed with consciousness and can enter into a Samādhi

---

[1] In the *Pieh-chuan* (another 'biography' of the Great Master of Ts'ao-ch'i—that is, of Hui-neng), and also in the current edition of the *T'an-ching*.

[2] Yüan-ts'e, according to the current edition of the *T'an-ching*.

like yourself. If, on the other hand, you are in a state of unconsciousness, plants and rocks can enter into a Samādhi.'

'Huang replied: "When I enter into a Samādhi, I am not conscious of either conditon."

'Yung said: "If you are not conscious of either condition, this is abiding in eternal Samādhi, and there can be neither entering into a Samādhi nor rising out of it."

'Huang made no reply. He asked: "You say you come from Neng, the great master. What instruction did you have under him?"

'Yung answered: "According to his instruction, no-tranquillization (ting-Samādhi), no-disturbance, no-sitting (tso), no-meditation (ch'an)—this is the Tathāgata's Dhyāna. The five Skandhas are not realities; the six objects of sense are by nature empty. It is neither quiet nor illuminating; it is neither real nor empty; it does not abide in the middle way; it is not-doing, it is no-effect-producing, and yet it functions with the utmost freedom: the Buddha-nature is all-inclusive.'

'This said, Huang at once realized the meaning of it and sighed: "These thirty years I have sat[1] to no purpose!" '

Another quotation from the *Life of Ts'ao-ch'i, the Great Master* will make the import of the above passages much clearer. The emperor Chung-tsung of the T'ang dynasty, learning of the spiritual attainment of Hui-neng, despatched a messenger to him, but he refused to come up to the capital. Whereupon the messenger, Hsieh-chien, asked to be instructed in the doctrine he espoused, saying: 'The great masters of Zen in the capital invariably teach their followers to practise meditation (ts'o-ch'an, dhyāna), for according to them no emancipation, no spiritual attainment is possible without it.'

To this Hui-neng replied: 'The Truth is understood by

[1] 'To sit' technically means 'to sit cross-legged in meditation', 'to practise Dhyāna', and it is generally used coupled with *ch'an* (*Zen* = *dhyāna*).

the mind (*hsin*), and not by sitting (*ts'o*) in meditation. According to the *Vajracchedikā*: "If people say that the Tathāgata sits or lies, they fail to understand my teaching. For the Tathāgata comes from nowhere and departs nowhither; and therefore he is called the Tathāgata ('Thus come')." Not coming from anywhere is birth, and not departing anywhither is death. Where there is neither birth nor death, there we have the purity-dhyāna of the Tathāgata. To see that all things are empty is to practise sitting (in meditation). . . . Ultimately, there is neither attainment nor realization; how much less sitting in meditation!'

Hui-neng further argued: 'As long as there is a dualistic way of looking at things there is no emancipation. Light stands against darkness; the passions stand against enlightenment. Unless these opposites are illuminated by Prajñā, so that the gap between the two is bridged, there is no understanding of the Mahāyāna. When you stay at one end of the bridge and are not able to grasp the oneness of the Buddha-nature, you are not one of us. The Buddha-nature knows neither decrease nor increase, whether it is in the Buddha or in common mortals. When it is within the passions, it is not defiled; when it is meditated upon, it does not thereby become purer. It is neither annihilated nor abiding; it neither comes not departs; it is neither in the middle nor at either end; it neither dies nor is born. It remains the same all the time, unchanged in all changes. As it is never born, it never dies. It is not that we replace death with life but that the Buddha-nature is above birth and death. The main point is not to think of things good and bad and thereby to be restricted, but to let the mind move on as it is in itself and perform its inexhaustible functions. This is the way to be in accord with the Mind-essence.'

Hui-neng's conception of Dhyāna, we can now see, was not that traditionally held by followers of the two vehicles.

His Dhyāna was not the art of tranquillizing the mind so that its inner essence, pure and undefiled, may come out of its casings. His Dhyāna was not the outcome of dualistically conceiving the Mind. The attempt to reach light by dispelling darkness is dualistic, and this will never lead the Yogin to the proper understanding of the mind. Nor is the attempt to annihilate the distinction the right one. Hui-neng therefore insisted on the identity of Dhyāna and Prajñā, for so long as Prajñā is kept apart from Dhyāna and Dhyāna from Prajñā, neither of the two is legitimately valued. One-sided Dhyāna is sure to tend towards quietism and death, as has abundantly been exemplified in the history of Zen and of Buddhism. For this reason we cannot treat Hui-neng's Dhyāna apart from his Prajñā.

The motive of the compiler of the *T'an-ching* was evidently to expound as the chief object of his work Hui-neng's idea of Prajñā, and to distinguish it from its traditional understanding. The title of the Tun-huang MS. unmistakably indicates this motive. It reads: 'The Sūtra of Mahā-prajñāpāramitā, of the Very Highest Mahāyāna (belonging to) the Southern School, and (Expounding its) Doctrine of Abrupt Awakening', while what follows reads something like a sub-title, 'The Platform Sermons (*sūtra=ching*) (containing) the Doctrine Given out by Hui-neng the Great Teacher, the Sixth Patriarch, at Tai-fan Ssu, of Shao-chou'. As these titles stand, it is difficult to tell which is the principal one. We know, however, that the Sūtra contains the sermons on Prajñā or Prajñāpāramitā as given out by Hui-neng, and that this doctrine belongs to the highest order of the Mahāyāna and of the Southern School, and is concerned with the Abrupt Doctrine which has come to characterize since the time of Hui-neng the teaching of all Zen schools.

After these titles, the opening passage acquaints us at once with the subject of the Sermon, perhaps the first ever given by Hui-neng, which deals with the doctrine of

Prajñāpāramitā. Indeed, Hui-neng himself begins his sermon with the exhortation: 'O my good friends, if you wish to see your minds purified, think of Mahāprajñāpāramitā.' And according to the text, Hui-neng remains silent for a while, cleansing his own heart. While I suspect his previous knowledge of the *Nirvāṇa Sūtra*, he at once, in the beginning of this Sermon, refers to the fact that he listened to the *Vajracchedikā Sūtra* before he came to Hung-jen. And, as we know, this is the Sūtra which became the principal authority for the teaching of Zen, and the one of all the Sūtras belonging to Prajñāpāramitā literature in which the doctrine of Prajñā is most concisely expounded. There is no doubt that Hui-neng was deeply connected with the Prajñāpāramitā from the outset of his career.

Even the teaching of Hung-jen, under whom Hui-neng studied Buddhism, is stated to have made specific reference to Prajñā. While it is doubtful whether Hung-jen was such an enthusiastic advocate of the doctrine of Prajñā as Hui-neng, at least the *T'an-ching* compiler took him as one. For Hung-jen's proclamation runs: '. . . Retire to your quarters, all of you, and by yourselves meditate on *Chih-hui* (the Chinese equivalent for Prajñā), and each compose a *gāthā* which treats of the nature of Prajñā in your original mind, and let me see it.' Does this not already anticipate Hui-neng? Hung-jen might have said something more, but this was at least what most impressed Hui-neng, and through him his compiler. It is also significant that Hung-jen refers to the *Vajracchedikā* when he expresses his intention to retain Shen-hsiu's poem on the wall where he first planned to have Lo-kung Feng's pictures of Zen history.

In fact, the doctrine of Prajñā is closely connected with that of Śūnyatā (emptiness), which is one of the most fundamental ideas of the Mahāyāna—so much so, indeed, that the latter altogether loses its significance when the Śūnyatā idea is dropped from its philosophy. The Hīnayāna also teaches the emptiness of all things, but its empti-

THE ZEN DOCTRINE OF NO-MIND

ness does not penetrate so deeply as the Mahāyāna's into the constitution of our knowledge. The two notions of the Hīnayāna and of the Mahāyāna regarding emptiness, we can say, are of different orders. When emptiness was raised to a higher order than formerly, the Mahāyāna began its history. To grasp this, Prajñā was needed, and naturally in the Mahāyāna Prajñā and Śūnyatā go hand in hand. Prajñā is no more mere knowledge dealing with relative objects; it is knowledge of the highest order permitted to the human mind, for it is the spark of the ultimate constituent of all things.

In the terminology of Chinese philosophy, *hsing* stands in most cases for the ultimate constituent, or that which is left after all that accidentally belongs to a thing is taken away from it. It may be questioned what is accidental and what is essential in the constitution of an individual object, but I will not stop to discuss the point, for I am more concerned with the exposition of the *T'an-ching* than with Chinese philosophy. Let us take it for granted that there is such a thing as *hsing*, which is something ultimate in the being of a thing or a person, though it must not be conceived as an individual entity, like a kernel or nucleus which is left when all the outer casings are removed, or like a soul which escapes from the body after death. *Hsing* means something without which no existence is possible, or thinkable as such. As its morphological construction suggests, it is 'a heart or mind which lives' within an individual. Figuratively, it may be called vital force.

The Chinese translators of the Sanskrit Buddhist texts adopted this character *hsing* to express the meaning contained in such terms as *buddhatā*, *dharmatā*, *svabhāva*, etc. *Buddhatā* is *fo-hsing*, 'Buddha-nature'; *dharmatā* is *fa-hsing*, 'nature or essence of all things'; and *svabhāva* is 'self-nature' or 'self-being'. In the *T'an-ching* we find *hsing* in the following combinations: *tzu-hsing*, 'self-nature'; *pen-hsing*, 'original nature'; *fo-hsing*, 'Buddha-nature'; *shih-*

hsing, 'realizing-nature'; *chen-hsing*, 'truth nature'; *miao-hsing*, 'mysterious nature'; *ching-hsing*, 'pure nature'; *ken-hsing*, 'root-nature'; *chiao-hsing*, 'enlightenment-nature'. Of these combinations the one which the reader will meet most frequently in Hui-neng is *tzu-hsing*, 'self-nature' or 'self-being', 'being-in-itself'.

And this *hsing* is defined by Hui-neng in the following manner: 'The *hsin* (mind or heart) is the dominion, *hsing* is the lord: the lord rules over his dominion, there is *hsing*, and there is the lord; *hsing* departs, and the lord is no more; *hsing* is and the body and mind (*hsin*) subsists, *hsing* is not and the body and mind is destroyed. The Buddha is to be made within *hsing* and not to be sought outside the body. . . .'[1]

In this, Hui-neng attempts to give us a clearer understanding of what he means by *hsing*. *Hsing* is the dominating force over our entire being; it is the principle of vitality, physical and spiritual. Not only the body but also the mind in its highest sense is active because of *hsing* being present in them. When *hsing* is no more, all is dead, though this does not mean that *hsing* is something apart from the body and mind, which enters into it to actuate it, and departs at the time of death. This mysterious *hsing*, however, is not a logical *a priori* but an actuality which can be experienced, and it is designated by Hui-neng as *tzu-hsing*, self-nature or self-being, throughout his *T'an-ching*.

Self-nature, otherwise expressed, is self-knowledge; it is not mere being but knowing. We can say that because of knowing itself, it is; knowing is being, and being is knowing. This is the meaning of the statement made by Hui-neng that: 'In original Nature itself there is Prajñā-knowledge, and because of this self-knowledge. Nature reflects itself in itself, which is self-illumination not to be expressed in words' (par. 30). When Hui-neng speaks of Prajñā-knowledge as if it is born of self-nature (par. 27),

[1] Par. 37.

40

this is due to the way of thinking which then prevailed, and often involves us in a complicated situation, resulting in the dualism of self-nature and Prajñā, which is altogether against the spirit of Hui-neng's Zen thought. We must, therefore, be on the watch when interpreting the *T'an-ching* in regard to the relation of Prajñā to self-nature.

However this may be, we have now come to Prajñā, which must be explained in the light of Dhyāna, whose Mahāyānist signification we have just examined. But before doing this I wish to say a few more words about self-nature and Prajñā. In Mahāyāna philosophy there are three concepts which have been resorted to by scholars to explain the relation between substance and its function. They are *tai* (body), *hsing* (form), and *yung* (use), which first appeared in *The Awakening of Faith in the Mahāyāna*, usually ascribed to Aśvaghosha. Body corresponds to substance, Form to appearance, and Use to function. The apple is a reddish, round-shaped object: this is its Form, in which it appeals to our senses. Form belongs to the world of senses, i.e. appearance. Its Use includes all that it does and stands for, its value, its utility, its function, and so on. Lastly, the Body of the apple is what constitutes its appleship, without which it loses its being, and no apple, even with all the appearances and functions ascribed to it, is an apple without it. To be a real object these three concepts, Body, Form, and Use, must be accounted for.

To apply these concepts to our object of discourse here, self-nature is the Body and Prajñā its Use, whereas there is nothing here corresponding to Form, because the subject does not belong to the world of form. There is the Buddha-nature, Hui-neng would argue, which makes up the reason of Buddhahood; and this is present in all beings, constituting their self-nature. The object of Zen discipline is to recognize it, and to be released from error, which are the passions. How is the recognition possible, one may inquire? It is possible because self-nature is self-knowledge. The Body is

41

no-body without its Use, and the Body is the Use. To be itself is to know itself. By using itself, its being is demonstrated, and this using is, in Hui-neng's terminology, 'seeing into one's own Nature'. Hands are no hands, have no existence, until they pick up flowers and offer them to the Buddha; so with legs, they are no legs, non-entities, unless their Use is set to work, and they walk over the bridge, ford the stream, and climb the mountain. Hence the history of Zen after Hui-neng developed this philosophy of Use to its fullest extent: the poor questioner was slapped, kicked, beaten, or called names to his utter bewilderment, and also to that of the innocent spectators. The initiative to this 'rough' treatment of the Zen students was given by Hui-neng, though he seems to have refrained from making any practical application of his philosophy of Use.

When we say, 'See into thy self-nature,' the seeing is apt to be regarded as mere perceiving, mere knowing, mere statically reflecting on self-nature, which is pure and undefiled, and which retains this quality in all beings as well as in all the Buddhas. Shen-hsiu and his followers undoubtedly took this view of the 'seeing'. But as a matter of fact, the seeing is an act, a revolutionary deed on the part of the human understanding whose functions have been supposed all the time to be logically analysing ideas, ideas sensed from their dynamic signification. The 'seeing', especially in Hui-neng's sense, was far more than a passive deed of looking at, a mere knowledge obtained from contemplating the purity of self-nature; the seeing with him was self-nature itself, which exposes itself before him in all nakedness, and functions without any reservation. Herein we observe the great gap between the Northern School of Dhyāna and the Southern School of Prajñā.

Shen-hsiu's school pays more attention to the Body aspect of self-nature, and tells its followers to concentrate their effects on the clearing up of consciousness, so as to see in it the reflection of self-nature, pure and undefiled.

They have evidently forgotten that self-nature is not a somewhat whose Body can be reflected on our consciousness in the way that a mountain can be seen reflected on the smooth surface of a lake. There is no such Body in self-nature, for the Body itself is the Use; besides the Use there is no Body. And by this Use is meant the Body's seeing itself in itself. With Shen-hsiu this self-seeing or Prajñā aspect of self-nature is altogether ignored. Hui-neng's position, on the contrary, emphasizes the Prajñā aspect we can know of self-nature.

This fundamental discrepancy between Hui-neng and Shen-hsiu in the conception of self-nature, which is the same thing as the Buddha-nature, has caused them to run in opposite directions as regards the practice of Dhyāna; that is, in the method of tso-ch'an (zazen in Japanese). Read the following gāthā[1] by Shen-hsiu:

> Our body is the Bodhi-tree,
> And our mind a mirror bright;
> Carefully we wipe them hour by hour
> And let no dust alight.

In the dust-wiping type of meditation (tso-ch'an, zazen) it is not easy to go further than the tranquillization of the mind; it is so apt to stop short at the stage of quiet contemplation, which is designated by Hui-neng 'the practice of keeping watch over purity'. At best it ends in ecstasy, self-absorption, a temporary suspension of consciousness. There is no 'seeing' in it, no knowing of itself, no active grasping of self-nature, no spontaneous functioning of it, no chen-hsing ('Seeing into Nature') whatever. The dust-wiping type is therefore the art of binding oneself with a self-created rope, an artificial construction which obstructs the way to emancipation. No wonder that Hui-neng and his followers attacked the Purity school.

[1] The T'an-ching (Kosjohi edition), par. 6.

The quietistic, dust-wiping, and purity-gazing type of meditation was probably one aspect of Zen taught by Hung-jen, who was the master of Hui-neng, Shen-hsiu, and many other. Hui-neng, who understood the real spirit of Zen most likely because he was not hampered by learning, and consequently by the conceptual attitude towards life, rightly perceived the danger of quietism, and cautioned his followers to avoid it by all means. But most other disciples of Hung-jen were more or less inclined to adopt quietism as the orthodox method of Dhyāna practice. Before Tao-i, popularly known as Ma-tsu, saw Huai-jang, of Nan-yueh, he was also a quiet-sitter who wanted to gaze at the pure nothingness of self-nature. He had been studying Zen under one of Hung-jen's disciples when he was still young. Even when he came up to Nan-yueh, he continued his old practice, keeping up his *tso-ch'an* ('sitting in meditation'). Hence the following discourse between himself and Huai-jang, who was one of the greatest disciples of Hui-neng.

Observing how assiduously Ma-tsu was engaged in practising *tso-ch'an* every day, Yuan Huai-jang said: 'Friend, what is your intention in practising *tso-ch'an*?' Ma-tsu said: 'I wish to attain Buddhahood.' Thereupon Huai-jang took up a brick and began to polish it. Ma-tsu asked: 'What are you engaged in?' 'I want to make a mirror of it.' 'No amount of polishing makes a mirror out of a brick.' Huai-jang at once retorted: 'No amount of practising *tso-ch'an* will make you attain Buddhahood.' 'What do I have to do then?' asked Ma-tsu. 'It is like driving a cart,' said Huai-jang. 'When it stops, what is the driver to do? To whip the cart, or to whip the ox?' Ma-tsu remained silent.

Another time Huai-jang said: 'Do you intend to be master of *tso-ch'an*, or do you intend to attain Buddhahood? If you wish to study Zen, Zen is neither in sitting cross-legged nor in lying down. If you wish to attain Buddahood by sitting cross-legged in meditation, the Buddha has no specified form. When the Dharma has no fixed abode, you cannot make any choice in it. If you attempt to attain Buddhahood by sitting cross-legged in meditation, this is murdering the Buddha. As long as you cling to this sitting posture you can never reach the Mind.'

Thus instructed, Ma-tsu felt as if he were taking a most delicious drink. Making bows, he asked: 'How should I prepare myself in order to be in accord with the Samādhi of formlessness?' The master said: 'Disciplining yourself in the study of Mind is like sowing seeds in the ground; my teaching in the Dharma is like pouring rain from above. When conditions are matured, you will see the Tao.[1]

Asked Ma-tsu again: 'The Tao has no form, and how can it be seen?'

The master replied: 'The Dharma-eye belonging to the Mind is able to see into the Tao. So it is with the Samādhi of formlessness.'

MA-TSU: 'Is it subject to completion and destruction?'

MASTER: 'If one applies to it such notions as completion and destruction, collection and dissipation, we can never have insight into it.'

In one sense Chinese Zen can be said to have really started with Ma-tsu and his contemporary Shih-tou, both of whom were the lineal descendants of Hui-neng. But before Ma-tsu was firmly established in Zen he was still under the influence of the dust-wiping and purity-gazing type of Dhyāna, applying himself most industriously to the practice of tso-ch'an, sitting cross-legged in meditation. He had no idea of the self-seeing type, no conception that self-nature which is self-being was self-seeing, that there was no Being besides Seeing which is Acting, that these three terms Being, Seeing, and Acting were synonymous and inter-changeable. The practice of Dhyāna was therefore to be furnished with an eye of Prajñā, and the two were to be considered one and not two separate concepts.

[1] Literally, 'Way', meaning truth, the Dharma, ultimate Reality.

To go back to Hui-neng. We now understand why he had to insist on the importance of Prajñā, and theorize on the oneness of Dhyāna and Prajñā. In the *T'an-ching* he opens his Sermon with the seeing into one's self-nature by means of Prajñā, with which every one of us, whether wise or ignorant, is endowed. Here he adopts the conventional way of expressing himself, as he is no original philosopher. In our own reasoning which we followed above, self-nature finds its own being when it sees itself, and this seeing takes place by Prajñā. But as Prajñā is another name given to self-nature when the latter sees itself, there is no Prajñā outside self-nature. The seeing (*chien*) is also called recognizing or understanding, or, better, experiencing (*wu* in Chinese and *satori* in Japanese). The character *Wu* is composed of 'heart' (or 'mind'), and 'mine'; that is, 'mine own heart', meaning 'to feel in my own heart', or 'to experience in my own mind'.

Self-nature is Prajñā, and also Dhyāna when it is viewed, as it were, statically or ontologically. Prajñā is more of epistemological signifiance. Now Hui-neng declares the oneness of Prajñā and Dhyāna. 'O good friends, in my teaching what is most fundamental is Dhyāna (*ting*) and Prajñā (*chin*). And, friends, do not be deceived and led to thinking that Dhyāna and Prajñā are separable. They are one, and not two. Dhyāna is the Body of Prajñā, and Prajñā is the Use of Dhyāna. When Prajñā is taken up, Dhyāna is in Prajñā; when Dhyāna is taken up, Prajñā is in it. When this is understood, Dhyāna and Prajñā go hand in hand in the practice (of meditation). O followers of the truth (*tao*), do not say that Dhyāna is first attained and then Prajñā awakened, or that Prajñā is first attained and then Dhyāna awakened; for they are separate. Those who advocate this view make a duality of the Dharma; they are those who affirm with the mouth and negate in the heart. They regard Dhyāna as distinct from Prajñā. But with those whose mouth and heart are in agreement, the inner and the outer are one, and Dhyāna and Prajñā are regarded as equal (*i.e.* as one).[1]

Hui-neng further illustrates the idea of this oneness by the relation between the lamp and its light. He says: 'It is like the lamp and its light. As there is a lamp, there is light; if no lamp, no light. The lamp is the Body of the light, and the light is the Use of the lamp. They are differently designated, but in substance they are one. The relation between Dhyāna and Prajñā is to be understood in like manner.'

This analogy of the lamp and its light is quite a favourite one with Zen philosophers. Shen-hui also makes use of it in his Sermon discovered by the author at the National Library of Peiping. In his *Sayings* (par. 19) we have Shen-hui's view on the oneness of Dhyāna and Prajñā, which was given as an answer to one of his questioners. 'Where no thoughts are awakened, and emptiness and nowhereness prevails, this is right Dhyāna. When this non-awakening of thought, emptiness, and nowhereness suffer themselves to be the object of perception, there is right Prajñā. Where this (mystery) takes place, we say that Dhyāna, taken up by itself, is the Body of Prajñā, and is not distinct from Prajñā, and is Prajñā itself; and further, that Prajñā, taken up by itself, is the Use of Dhyāna, and is not distinct from Dhyāna, and is Dhyāna itself. (Indeed) when Dhyāna is to be taken up by itself, there is no Dhyāna; when Prajñā is to be taken up by itself, there is no Prajñā. Why? Because (Self-) nature is suchness, and this is what is meant by the oneness of Dhyāna and Prajñā.'

In this, Hui-neng and Shen-hui are of the same view. But being still too abstract for the ordinary understanding, it may be found difficult to grasp what is really meant by it. In the following, Shen-hui is more concrete or more accessible in his statement.

Wang-wei was a high government officer greatly in-

[1] The *T'an-ching* (Koshoji edition), par. 14.

terested in Buddhism, and when he learned of the disagreement between Shen-hui and Hui-ch'eng, who was
evidently a follower of Shen-hsiu, regarding Dhyāna and
Prajñā, he asked Shen-hui: 'Why this disagreement?'

Shen-hui answered: 'The disagreement is due to Ch'eng's
holding the view that Dhyāna is to be practised first and
that it is only after its attainment that Prajñā is awakened.
But according to my view, the very moment I am conversing
with you, there is Dhyāna, there is Prajñā, and they are the
same. According to the *Nirvāṇa Sūtra*, when there is more
of Dhyāna and less of Prajñā, this helps the growth of
ignorance; when there is more of Prajñā and less of Dhyāna,
this helps the growth of false views; but when Dhyāna and
Prajñā are the same, this is called seeing into the Buddha-
nature. For this reason, I say we cannot come to an agreement.'

WANG: 'When are Dhyāna and Prajñā said to be the same?'
SHEN-HUI: 'We speak of Dhyāna, but as to its Body there
is nothing attainable in it. Prajñā is spoken of when it is seen
that this Body is unattainable, remaining perfectly quiescent
and serene all the time, and yet functioning mysteriously in
ways beyond calculation. Herein we observe Dhyāna and
Prajñā to be identical.'

Both Hui-neng and Shen-hsiu lay stress on the signi-
ficance of the Prajñā-eye, which, being turned on itself,
sees into the mysteries of Self-nature. The unattainable is
attained, the eternally serene is perceived, and Prajñā
identifies itself with Dhyāna in its varied functionings.
Therefore, while Shen-hui is talking with Wang-wei,
Shen-hui declares that in this talking Dhyāna as well as
Prajñā is present, that this talking itself is Prajñā and
Dhyāna. By this he means that Prajñā is Dhyāna and
Dhyāna is Prajñā. If we say that only while sitting cross-
legged in meditation there is Dhyāna, and that when this
type of sitting is completely mastered, there for the first
time Prajñā is awakened, we effect a complete severance

48

of Prajñā and Dhyāna, which is a dualism always ab-horred by Zen followers. Whether moving or not-moving, whether talking or not-talking, there musy be Dhyāna in it, which is ever-abiding Dhyāna. Again, we must say that being is seeing and seeing is acting, that there is no being, i.e. Self-nature, without seeing and acting, and that Dhyāna is Dhyāna only when it is at the same time Prajñā. The following is a quotation from Ta-chu Hui-hai, who was a disciple of Ma-tsu:

Q.: 'When there is no word, no discourse, this is Dhyāna; but when there are words and discourses, can this be called Dhyāna?'
A.: 'When I speak of Dhyāna, it has no relationship to discoursing or not discoursing; my Dhyāna is ever-abiding Dhyāna. Why? Because Dhyāna is all the while in Use. Even when words are uttered, discoursing goes on, or when discriminative reasoning prevails, there is Dhyāna in it, for all is Dhyāna.

'When a mind, thoroughly understanding the emptiness of all things, faces forms, it at once realizes their emptiness. With it emptiness is there all the time, whether it faces forms or not, whether it discourses or not, whether it discriminates or not. This applies to everything which belongs to our sight, hearing, memory, and consciousness generally. Why is it so? Because all things in their self-nature are empty; and wherever we go we find this emptiness. As all is empty, no attachment takes place; and on account of this non-attachment there is a simultaneous Use (of Dhyāna and Prajñā). The Bodhisattva always knows how to make Use of emptiness, and thereby he attains the Ultimate. Therefore it is said that by the oneness of Dhyāna and Prajñā is meant Emancipation.'

That Dhyāna has nothing to do with mere sitting cross-legged in meditation, as is generally supposed by outsiders, or as has been maintained by Shen-hsiu and his school ever since the days of Hui-neng, is here asserted in a most unmistakable manner. Dhyāna is not quietism, nor is it tranquillization; it is rather acting, moving, performing deeds, seeing, hearing, thinking, remembering; Dhyāna is attained where there is, so to speak, no Dhyāna practised; Dhyāna is Prajñā, and Prajñā is Dhyāna, for they are one. This is one of the themes constantly stressed by all the Zen masters following Hui-neng.

Ta-chu Hui-hai continues: 'Let me give you an illustration, that your doubt may be cleared up and you may feel refreshed. It is like a brightly-shining mirror reflecting images on it. When the mirror does this, does the brightness suffer in any way? No, it does not. Does it then suffer when there are no images reflected? No, it does not. Why? Because the Use of the bright mirror is free from affections, and therefore its reflection is never obscured. Whether images are reflected or not, there are no changes in its brightness. Why? Because that which is free from affections knows no change in all conditions.

'Again, it is like the sun illumining the world. Does the light suffer any change? No, it does not. How, when it does not illumine the world? There are no changes in it, either. Why? Because the light is free from affections, and therefore whether it illumines objects or not, the unaffected sunlight is ever above change.

'Now the illumining light is Prajñā, and unchangeability is Dhyāna. The Bodhisattva uses Dhyāna and Prajñā in their oneness, and thereby attains enlightenment. Therefore it is said that by using Dhyāna and Prajñā in their oneness emancipation is meant. Let me add that to be free from affections means the absence of the passions and not that of the noble aspirations (which are free from the dualistic conception of existence).'

In Zen philosophy, in fact in all Buddhist philosophy, no distinctions are made between logical and psychological terms, and the one turns into the other quite readily. From the viewpoint of life no such distinctions can exist, for here logic is psychology and psychology is logic. For this reason Ta-chu Hui-hai's psychology becomes logic with Shen-hui, and they both refer to the same experience. We read in Shen-hui's *Sayings* (par. 32): 'A bright mirror is set up on a high stand; its illumination reaches the ten-thousand things, and they are all reflected in it. The masters are wont to consider this phenomenon most wonderful. But as far as my school is concerned it is not to be considered wonderful. Why? As to this bright mirror, its illumination reaches the ten-thousand things, and these ten-thousand things are not reflected in it. This is what I would declare to be most wonderful. Why? The Tathāgata discriminates all things with non-discriminating Prajñā (*chih*). If he has any discriminating mind, do you think he could discriminate all things?'

The Chinese term for 'discrimination' is *fen-pieh*, which is a translation of the Sanskrit *vikalpa*, one of the important Buddhist terms used in various Sūtras and Śastras. The original meaning of the Chinese characters is 'to cut and divide with a knife', which exactly corresponds to the etymology of the Sanskrit *viklp*. By 'discrimination', therefore, is meant analytical knowledge, the relative and discursive understanding which we use in our everyday worldly intercourse and also in our highly speculative thinking. For the essence of thinking is to analyse—that is, to discriminate; the sharper the knife of dissection, the more subtle the resulting speculation. But according to the Buddhist way of thinking, or rather according to the Buddhist experience, this power of discrimination is based on non-discriminating Prajñā (*chih* or *chih-hui*). This is what is most fundamental in the human understanding, and it is with this that we are able to have an insight into the Self-nature possessed by us all, which is also known as Buddha-nature. Indeed, Self-nature is Prajñā itself, as has been repeatedly stated above. And this non-discriminating Prajñā is what is 'free from affections', which is the term Ta-chu Hui-hai uses in characterizing the mind-mirror.

Thus 'non-discriminating Prajñā', 'to be free from affections', 'from the first not a thing is'—all these expressions point to the same source, which is the fountainhead of Zen experience.

Now the question is: How is it possible for the human mind to move from discrimination to non-discrimination, from affections to affectionlessness, from being to non-being, from relativity to emptiness, from the ten-thousand things to the contentless mirror-nature or Self-nature, or, Buddhistically expressed, from *mayoi* (*mi* in Chinese) to *satori* (*wu*)?[1] How this movement is possible is the greatest mystery not only in Buddhism but in all religion and philosophy. So long as this world, as conceived by the human mind, is a realm of opposites, there is no way to escape from it and to enter into a world of emptiness where all opposites are supposed to merge. The wiping-off of the multitudes known as the ten-thousand things in order to see into the mirror-nature itself is an absolute impossibility. Yet Buddhists all attempt to achieve it.

Philosophically stated, the question is not properly put. It is not the wiping-off of the multitudes, it is not moving from discrimination to non-discrimination, from relativity to emptiness, etc. Where the wiping-off process is accepted, the idea is that when the wiping-off is completed, the mirror shows its original brightness, and therefore the process is continuous on one line of movement. But the fact is that the wiping itself is the work of the original brightness. The 'original' has no reference to time, in the sense that the mirror was once, in its remote past, pure and undefiled, and

---

[1] *Mayoi* means 'standing on a cross-road', and not knowing which way to go; that is, 'going astray', 'not being in the way of truth'. It stands contrasted with *satori* (*wu*), which is the right understanding, realization of truth.

that as it is no more so, it must be polished up and its original brightness be restored. The brightness is there all the time, even when it is thought to be covered with dust and not reflecting objects as it should. The brightness is not something to be restored; it is not something appearing at the completion of the procedure; it has never departed from the mirror. This is what is meant when the *T'an-ching* and other Buddhist writings declare the Buddha-nature to be the same in all beings, including the ignorant as well as the wise.

As the attainment of the Tao does not involve a continuous movement from error to truth, from ignorance to enlightenment, from *mayoi* to *satori*, the Zen masters all proclaim that there is no enlightenment whatever which you can claim to have attained. If you say you have attained something, this is the surest proof that you have gone astray. Therefore, not to have is to have; silence is thunder; ignorance is enlightenment; the holy disciples of the Purity-path go to hell while the precept-violating Bhikshus attain Nirvāṇa; the wiping-off means dirt-accumulating; all these paradoxical sayings—and Zen literature is filled with them—are no more than so many negations of the continuous movement from discrimination to non-discrimination, from affectibility to non-affectibility, etc., etc.

The idea of a continuous movement fails to account for the facts, first, that the moving process stops at the originally bright mirror, and makes no further attempt to go on indefinitely, and secondly, that the pure nature of the mirror suffers itself to be defiled, i.e. that from one object comes another object absolutely contradicting it. To put this another way: absolute negation is needed, but can it be possible when the process is continuous? Here is the reason why Hui-neng persistently opposes the view cherished by his opponents. He does not espouse the doctrine of continuity which is the Gradual School of Shen-hsiu. All those who hold the view of a continuous movement belong to the latter. Hui-neng, on the other hand, is the champion of the Abrupt School. According to this school the movement from *mayoi* to *satori* is abrupt and not gradual, discrete and not continuous.

That the process of enlightenment is abrupt means that there is a leap, logical and psychological, in the Buddhist experience. The logical leap is that the ordinary process of reasoning stops short, and what has been considered irrational is perceived to be perfectly natural, while the psychological leap is that the borders of consciousness are overstepped and one is plunged into the Unconscious which is not, after all, unconscious. This process is discrete, abrupt, and altogether beyond calculation; this is 'Seeing into one's Self-nature'. Hence the following statement by Hui-neng:

'O friends, while under Jen the Master I had a *satori* (*wu*) by just once listening to his words, and abruptly saw into the original nature of Suchness. This is the reason why I wish to see this teaching propagated, so that seekers of the truth may also abruptly have an insight into Bodhi, see each by himself what his mind (*hsin*) is, what his original nature is. . . . All the Buddhas of the past, present, and future, and all the Sūtras belonging to the twelve divisions are in the self-nature of each individual, where they were from the first. . . . There is within oneself that which knows, and thereby one has a *satori*. If there rises an erroneous thought, false-hoods and perversions obtain; and no outsiders, however wise, are able to instruct such people, who are, indeed, beyond help. But if there takes place an illumination by means of genuine Prajñā, all falsehoods vanish in an in-stant. If one's self-nature is understood, one's *satori* is enough to make one rise to a state of Buddhahood. O friends, when there is a Prajñā illumination, the inside as well as the outside becomes thoroughly translucent, and a man knows by himself what his original mind is, which is no more than emancipation. When emancipation is obtained, it is the Prajñā-samādhi, and when this Prajñā-samādhi is understood, there is realized a state of *mu-nen* (*wu-nien*), "thought-less-ness".'

The teaching of abrupt *satori* is then fundamental in the Southern School of Hui-neng. And we must remember that this abruptness or leaping is not only psychological, but dialectical.

Prajñā is really a dialectical term denoting that this special process of knowing, known as 'abruptly seeing', or 'seeing at once', does not follow general laws of logic; for when Prajñā functions one finds oneself all of a sudden, as if by a miracle, facing Śūnyatā, the emptiness of all things. This does not take place as the result of reasoning, but when reasoning has been abandoned as futile, and psychologically when the will-power is brought to a finish.

The Use of Prajñā contradicts everything that we may conceive of things worldly; it is altogether of another order than our usual life. But this does not mean that Prajñā is something altogether disconnected with our life and thought, something that is to be given to us by a miracle from some unknown and unknowable source. If this were the case, Prajñā would be of no possible use to us, and there would be no emancipation for us. It is true that the functioning of Prajñā is discrete, and interrupting to the progress of logical reasoning, but all the time it underlies it, and without Prajñā we cannot have any reasoning whatever. Prajñā is at once above and in the process of reasoning. This is a contradiction, formally considered, but in truth this contradiction itself is made possible because of Prajñā.

That almost all religious literature is filled with contradictions, absurdities, paradoxes, and impossibilities, and demands to believe them, to accept them, as revealed truths, is due to the fact that religious knowledge is based on the working of Prajñā. Once this viewpoint of Prajñā is gained, all the essential irrationalities found in religion become intelligible. It is like appreciating a fine piece of brocade. On the surface there is an almost bewildering confusion of beauty, and the connoisseur fails to trace the intricacies of the threads. But as soon as it is turned over all the intricate beauty and skill is revealed. Prajñā consists in this turning-over. The eye has hitherto followed the surface of the cloth, which is indeed the only side ordinarily allowed us to survey. Now, the cloth is abruptly turned over; the course of the eyesight is suddenly interrupted; no continuous gazing is possible. Yet by this interruption, or rather disruption, the whole scheme of life is suddenly grasped; there is the 'seeing into one's self-nature'.

The point I wish to make here is that the reason side has been there all the time, and that it is because of this unseen side that the visible side has been able to display its multiple beauty. This is the meaning of discriminative reasoning being always based on non-discriminating Prajñā; this is the meaning of the statement that the mirror-nature of emptiness (*śūnyatā*) retains all the time its original brightness, and is never once beclouded by anything outside which is reflected on it; this is again the meaning of all things being such as they are in spite of their being arranged in time and space and subject to the so-called laws of nature.

This something conditioning all things and itself not being conditioned by anything assumes various names as it is viewed from different angles. Spatially, it is called 'formless' against all that can be subsumed under form; temporarily, it is 'non-abiding', as it moves on for ever, not being cut up into pieces called thoughts and as such detained and retained as something abiding; psychologically it is 'the unconscious' (*wu-nien*=*mu-nen*) in the sense that all our conscious thoughts and feelings grow out of the Unconscious, which is Mind (*hsin*), or Self-nature (*tzu-hsing*).

As Zen is more concerned with experience and hence with psychology, let us go further into the idea of the Unconscious. The original Chinese is *Wu-nien* (*mu-nen*) or *Wu-hsin* (*mu-shin*), and literally means 'no-thought', or 'no-mind'. But *nien* or *hsin* means more than thought or mind. This I have elsewhere explained in detail. It is rather difficult to give here an exact English equivalent for *nien* or *hsin*. Hui-neng and Shen-hui use principally *nien* instead of *hsin*, but there are other Zen masters who prefer *hsin* to *nien*. In point of fact, the two designate the same experience: *wu-nien* and *wu-hsin* point to the same state of consciousness.

The character *hsin* originally symbolizes the heart as the organ of affection, but has later come to indicate also the seat of thinking and willing. *Hsin* has thus a broad connotation, and may be taken largely to correspond to consciousness. *Wu-nien* is 'no-consciousness', thus the unconscious. The character *nien* has *chien* 'now', over the heart, and might originally have meant anything present at the moment in consciousness. In Buddhist literature, it frequently stands for the Sanskrit *Kṣaṇa*, meaning 'a thought', 'a moment regarded as a unit of time', 'an instant'; but as a psychological term it is generally used to denote 'memory', 'intense thinking', and 'consciousness'. *Wu-nien* thus also means 'the unconscious'.

What, then, do the Zen masters mean by 'the unconscious'?

It is evident that in Zen Buddhism the unconscious is not a psychological term either in a narrower or in a broader sense. In modern psychology the scientists refer to the unconscious as underlying consciousness, where a large mass of psychological factors are kept buried under one name or another. They appear in the field of consciousness sometimes in response to a call, and therefore by a conscious effort, but quite frequently unexpectedly and in a disguised form. To define this unconsciousness baffles the psychologists just because it is the unconscious. The fact is, however, that it is a reservoir of mysteries and a source of superstitions. And for this reason the concept of the unconscious has been abused by unscrupulous religionists, and some people hold that Zen is also guilty of this crime. The accusation is justifiable if Zen philosophy is no more than a psychology of the unconscious in its ordinary definition.

According to Hui-neng, the concept of the unconscious is the foundation of Zen Buddhism. In fact he proposes three concepts as constituting Zen, and the unconscious is one of them; the other two are 'formlessness' (*wu-hsing*) and 'non-abiding' (*wu-chu*). Hui-neng continues: 'By formlessness is meant to be in form and yet to be detached from it; by the unconscious is meant to have thoughts and yet not to have them; as to non-abiding it is the primary nature of man.'

His further definition of the unconscious is: 'O good friends, not to have the Mind tainted while in contact with all conditions of life,[1]—this is to be Unconscious. It is to be always detached from objective conditions in one's own consciousness, not to let one's mind be roused by coming in contact with objective conditions. . . . O good friends, why is the Unconscious established as fundamental? There are some people with confused ideas who talk about seeing into their own nature, but whose consciousness is not liberated from objective conditions, and (my teaching) is only for the sake of such people. Not only are they conscious of objective conditions, but they contrive to cherish false views, from which all worldly worries and vagaries rise. But in self-nature there is from the first not a thing which is attainable. If anything attainable is here conceived, fortune and misfortune will be talked about; and

---

[1] *Ching* in Chinese. It means 'boundaries', 'an area enclosed by them', 'environment', 'objective world'. In its technical sense it stands contrasted with *hsin*, mind.

this is no more than worrying and giving oneself up to vagaries. Therefore in my teaching, unconsciousness is established as fundamental.

'O good friends, what is there for *wu* (of *wu-nien*, unconsciousness) to negate? And what is there for *nien* to be conscious of? *Wu* is to negate the notion of two forms (dualism), and to get rid of a mind which worries over things, while *nien* means to become conscious of the primary nature of Suchness (*tathatā*); for Suchness is the Body of Consciousness, and Consciousness is the Use of Suchness. It is the self-nature of Suchness to become conscious of itself; it is not the eye, ear, nose, and tongue that is conscious; as Suchness has (self-) nature, consciousness rises in it; if there were no Suchness, then eye and ear, together with forms and sounds, would be destroyed. In the self-nature of Suchness there rises consciousness; while in the six senses there is seeing, hearing, remembering, and recognizing; the self-nature is not tainted by objective conditions of all kinds; the true nature moves with perfect freedom, discriminating all forms in the objective world and inwardly unmoved in the first principle.'

While it is difficult and often misleading to apply the modern way of thinking to those ancient masters, especially masters of Zen, we must to a certain extent hazard this application, for otherwise there will be no chance of even a glimpse into the secrets of Zen experience. For one thing, we have what Hui-neng calls self-nature, which is the Buddhanature of the *Nirvāṇa Sūtra* and other Mahāyāna writings. This self-nature in terms of the *Prajñāpāramitā* is Suchness (*tathatā*), and Emptiness (*śūnyatā*). Suchness means the Absolute, something which is not subject to laws of relativity, and therefore which cannot be grasped by means of form. Suchness is thus formlessness. In Buddhism, form (*rūpa*) stands against no-form (*arūpa*), which is the unconditioned. This unconditioned, formless, and consequently

59

unattainable is Emptiness (*śūnyatā*). Emptiness is not a negative idea, nor does it mean mere privation, but as it is not in the realm of names and forms it is called emptiness, or nothingness, or the Void.

Emptiness is thus unattainable. 'Unattainable' means to be beyond perception, beyond grasping, for emptiness is on the other side of being and non-being. All our relative knowledge is concerned with dualities. But if emptiness is absolutely beyond all human attempts to take hold of in any sense whatever, it has no value for us; it does not come into the sphere of human interest; it is really non-existent, and we have nothing to do with it. But the truth is otherwise. Emptiness constantly falls within our reach; it is always with us and in us, and conditions all our knowledge, all our deeds, and is our life itself. It is only when we attempt to pick it up and hold it forth as something before our eyes that it eludes us, frustrates all our efforts, and vanishes like vapour. We are ever lured towards it, but it proves a will-o'-the-wisp.

It is Prajñā which lays its hands on Emptiness, or Suchness, or self-nature. And this laying-hands-on is not what it seems. This is self-evident from what has already been said concerning things relative. Inasmuch as self-nature is beyond the realm of relativity, its being grasped by Prajñā cannot mean a grasping in its ordinary sense. The grasping must be no-grasping, a paradoxical statement which is inevitable. To use Buddhist terminology, this grasping is accomplished by non-discrimination; that is, by non-discriminating discrimination. The process is abrupt, discrete, an act of the conscious; not an unconscious act but an act rising from self-nature itself, which is the Unconscious.

Hui-neng's Unconscious is thus fundamentally different from the psychologists' Unconscious. It has a metaphysical connotation. When Hui-neng speaks of the Unconscious in Consciousness, he steps beyond psychology; he is not referring even to the Unconscious forming the basis of consciousness, which goes to the remotest part when the mind has not yet evolved, the mind being still in a state of mere sustenance. Nor is Hui-neng's Unconscious a kind of world-spirit which is found floating on the surface of chaos. It is timeless, and yet contains all time with its minutest periods as well as all its aeons.

Shen-hui's definition of the Unconscious which we have in his *Sayings* (par. 14) will shed further light on the subject. When preaching to others on the *Prajñāpāramitā* he says: 'Be not attached to form. Not to be attached to form means Suchness. What is meant by Suchness? It means the Unconscious. What is the Unconscious? It is not to think of being and non-being; it is not to think of good and bad; it is not to think of having limits or not having limits; it is not to think of measurements (or of non-measurements); it is not to think of enlightenment, nor is it to think of being enlightened; it is not to think of Nirvāṇa, nor is it to think of attaining Nirvāna: this is the Unconscious. The Unconscious is no other than Prajñāpāramitā itself. Prajñāpāramitā is no other than the Samādhi of Oneness.

'O friends, if there are among you some who are still in the stage of learners, let them turn their illumination (upon the source of consciousness) whenever thoughts are awakened in their minds. When the awakened mind is dead, the conscious illumination vanishes by itself—this is the Unconscious. This Unconscious is absolutely free from all conditions, for if there are any conditions it cannot be known as the Unconscious.

'O friends, that which sees truly sounds the depths of the Dharmadhātu, and this is known as the Samādhi of Oneness. Therefore, it is said in the *Smaller Prajñāpāramitā*: "O good men, this is Prajñāpāramitā, that is to say, not to have any (conscious) thoughts in regard to things. As we live in that which is unconscious, this golden-coloured body, with the thirty-two marks of supreme manhood, emits rays of great effulgence, contains Prajñā altogether beyond thinking, is endowed with all the highest Samādhis attained by the Buddhas, and with incomparable knowledge. All the merits (accruing from the Unconscious) cannot be recounted by the Buddhas, much less by the Śrāvakas and the Pratyeka-Buddhas." He who sees the Unconscious is not tainted by the six senses; he who sees the Unconscious is enabled to turn towards the Buddha-knowledge; he who sees the Unconscious is called Reality; he who sees the Unconscious is the Middle Way and the first truth; he who sees the Unconscious is furnished at once with merits of the Gangā; he who sees the Unconscious is able to produce all things; he who sees the Unconscious is able to take in all things.'

This view of the Unconscious is thoroughly confirmed by Ta-chu Hui-hai, a chief disciple of Ma-tsu, in his *Essential Teaching of the Abrupt Awakening*: 'The Unconscious means to have no-mind in all circumstances, that is to say, not to be determined by any conditions, not to have any affections or hankerings. To face all objective conditions, and yet to be eternally free from any form of stirring, this is the Unconscious. The Unconscious is thus known as to be truly conscious of itself. But to be conscious of consciousness is a false form of the Unconscious. Why? The Sūtra states that to make people become conscious of the six vijñānas is to have the wrong consciousness; to cherish the six vijñānas is false; where a man is free from the six vijñānas, he has the right consciousness.'

'To see the Unconscious' does not mean any form of self-consciousness, nor is to sink into a state of ecstasy or indifference or apathy, where all traces of ordinary consciousness are wiped out. 'To see the Unconscious' is to be conscious and yet to be unconscious of self-nature. Because self-nature is not to be determined by the logical category of being and non-being, to be so determined means to bring self-nature into the realm of empirical psychology, in which it ceases to be what it is in itself. If the Unconscious, on the other hand, means the loss of consciousness, it then spells death, or at best a temporary suspension of life itself. But this is impossible inasmuch as self-nature is the Mind itself. This is the sense of the following passage which we come across everywhere in the *Prajñāpāramitā* and other Mahāyāna Sūtras: 'To be unconscious in all circumstances is possible because the ultimate nature of all things is emptiness, and because there is after all not a form which one can say one has laids hands on. This unattainability of all things is Reality itself, which is the most exquisite form of the Tathāgata.' The Unconscious is thus the ultimate reality, the true form, the most exquisite body of Tathāgatahood. It is certainly not a hazy abstraction, not a mere conceptual postulate, but a living experience in its deepest sense.

Further descriptions of the Unconscious from Shen-hui are as follows:

'To see into the Unconscious is to understand self-nature; to understand self-nature is not to take hold of anything; not to take hold of anything is the Tathāgata's Dhyāna. . . . Self-nature is from the first thoroughly pure, because its Body is not to be taken hold of. To see it thus is to be on the same standing with the Tathāgata, to be detached from all forms, to have all the vagaries of falsehood at once quieted, to equip oneself with merits of absolute stainlessness, to attain true emancipation, etc.'

'The nature of Suchness is our original Mind, of which we are conscious; and yet there is neither the one who is conscious nor that of which there is a consciousness.'

'To those who see the Unconscious, karma ceases to function, and what is the use for them to cherish an erroneous thought and to try to destroy karma by means of confusion?'

'To go beyond the dualism of being and non-being,

and again to love the track of the Middle Way—this is the Unconscious. The Unconscious means to be conscious of the absolutely one; to be conscious of the absolutely one means to have all-knowledge, which is Prajñā. Prajñā is the Tathāgata-Dhyāna.'

We are back again here at the relationship of Prajñā and Dhyāna. This is in fact one of the recurring subjects in the philosophy of Buddhism, and we cannot get away from it, especially in the study of Zen. The difference between Shen-hsiu's and Hui-neng's school is no more than the difference which exists between them in regard to this relationship. Shen-hsiu approaches the problem from the point of view of Dhyāna, while Hui-neng upholds Prajñā as the most important thing in the grasping of Zen. The latter tells us first of all 'to see' self-nature, which means to wake up in the Unconscious; Shen-hsiu, on the other hand, advises us 'to sit in meditation', so that all our passions and disturbing thoughts may be quieted, and the inherent purity of self-nature shine out by itself. These two tendencies have been going on side by side in the history of Zen thought, probably due to the two psychological types to be found in us, intuitive and moral, intellectual and practical.

Those who emphasize Prajñā, like Hui-neng and his school, tend to identify Dhyāna with Prajñā, and insist on an abrupt, instantaneous awakening in the Unconscious. This awakening in the Unconscious may be, logically speaking, a contradiction, but as Zen has another world in which to live its own life, it does not mind contradictory expressions and continues to use its peculiar phraseology.

Hui-neng's school thus objects to Shen-hsiu's on the grounds that those who spend their time in sitting cross-legged in meditation, trying to realize the state of tranquillity, are seekers after some tangible attainment; they are upholders of the doctrine of original purity, which they consider to be something intellectually demonstrable; they are gazers at a special object which can be picked up among other relative objects and shown to others as one points at the moon; they cling to this specific object as something most precious, forgetting that this clinging degrades the value of their cherished object because it is thereby brought down to the same order of being as themselves; because of this clinging to it and abiding in it, they cherish a certain definite state of consciousness as the ultimate point they should attain; therefore they are never truly emancipated, they have not cut the last string which keeps them still on this side of existence.

According to Hui-neng's Prajñā school, Prajñā and Dhyāna become identical in the Unconscious, for when there is an awakening in the Unconscious, this is no awakening, and the Unconscious remains all the time in Dhyāna, serene and undisturbed.

The awakening is never to be taken for an attainment or for an accomplishment as the result of such strivings. As there is no attainment in the awakening of Prajñā in the Unconscious, there is no abiding in it either. This is the point most emphatically asserted in all the Prajñāpāramitā Sūtras. No attainment, and therefore no clinging, no abiding, which means abiding in the Unconscious or abiding in non-abiding.

In Ta-chu Hui-hai we have this dialogue:

Q. 'What is meant by the simultaneous functioning of the Triple Discipline?'

A. 'To be pure and undefiled is Śīla (precept). The mind unmoved remaining ever serene in all conditions is Dhyāna (meditation). To perceive the mind unmoved, and yet to raise no thoughts as to its immovability; to perceive the mind pure and undefiled, and yet to raise no thoughts as to its purity; to discriminate what is bad from what is good, and yet to feel no defilement by them, and to be absolute master of oneself: this is known as Prajñā. When one perceives thus that Sīla, Dhyāna, and Prajñā are all beyond attainability, one at once realizes that there is no discrimination to be made between them, and that they are of one and the same Body. This is the simultaneous functioning of the Triple Discipline.'

Q. 'When the mind abides in purity, is this not clinging to it?'

A. 'When abiding in purity, one may have no thoughts of abiding in it, and then one is said not to be clinging to it.'

Q. 'When the mind abides in emptiness, is this not clinging to it?'

A. 'When one has thoughts as to thus abiding, there is a clinging in one.'

Q. 'When the mind abides in the non-abiding, is this not clinging to the non-abiding?'

A. 'When one cherishes no thoughts as to emptiness, there is no clinging. If you wish to understand when the mind comes to realize the moment of non-abiding, sit in the right meditation posture, and purge your mind thoroughly of thoughts—thoughts about all things, thoughts about goodness and badness of things. Events past are already past; therefore have no thoughts of them, and your mind is disconnected from the past. Thus past events are done away with.[1] Present events are already here before you; then have no attachment to them. Not to have attachment means not to rouse any feeling of hate or love. Your mind is then disconnected from the present, and the events before your eyes are done away with. When the past, present, and future are thus in no way taken in, they are completely done away with. When thoughts come and go, do not follow them, and your pursuing mind is cut off. When abiding (with thoughts) do not tarry in them, and your

[1] Events to come áre not yet come, and you need not worry about them; do not seek for them. Thus your mind is disconnected from the future.

66

abiding mind is cut off. When thus freed from abiding (with thoughts), you are said to be abiding with the non-abiding. If you have a thoroughly clear perception of yourself, you may remain abiding with thoughts, and yet what remains abiding is thoughts (and as to your Unconscious), it has neither an abiding place nor a non-abiding place. If you have a thoroughly clear perception as to the mind having no abiding place anywhere, this is known as having a thoroughly clear perception of one's own being. This very Mind which has no abiding place anywhere is the Buddha-Mind itself; it is called Emancipation-Mind, Enlightenment-Mind, the Unborn Mind, and Emptiness of Materiality and Ideality. It is what is designated in the sūtras as Recognition of the Unborn. . . . All this is understood when one has the Unconscious in evidence anywhere.'

The doctrine of the Unconscious as expounded here is, psychologically translated, that of absolute passivity or absolute obedience. It may also be represented as the teaching of humility. Our individual consciousness merged into the Unconscious must become like the body of a dead man, as used by St. Francis of Assisi to illustrate his idea of the perfect and highest obedience.

To make oneself like a corpse or a piece of wood or rock, though from a very different standpoint, seems to have been a favourite simile with Zen Buddhists too.

In Huang-po Hsi-yun we have this:

Q. 'What is meant by worldly knowledge?'

A. 'What is the use of involving yourself in such complexities? (The Mind) is thoroughly pure from the first, and no wordy discussions are needed about it. Only have no mind of any kind, and this is known as undefiled knowledge. In your daily life, whether walking or standing, sitting or lying, let not your speech of any nature be attached to things of the world; then whatever words you utter and in whichever way your eyes blink, they are all of undefiled knowledge. The world is at present on the way to general decline, and most Zen students are attached to things material and worldly. What concern have they after all with Mind? Let your mind be like vacuity of space, like a chip of dead wood and a piece of stone, like cold ashes and burnt-out coal. When this is done, you may feel some correspondence (to the true Mind). If otherwise, some day you will surely be taken to task by the old man of the other world. . . .'

Ignatius Loyola's recommendation of obedience as the foundation of his Order differs naturally in spirit from the idea of the Zen masters' recommendation of what may be called absolute indifference. They are indifferent to things happening to them, because they consider them as not touching the Unconscious which lies at the back of their surface consciousness. As they hold themselves intimately to the Unconscious, all the outer happenings, including what is popularly known as belonging to one's consciousness, are like shadows. Being so, they are suffered to assail the Zen master, while his Unconscious remains undisturbed. This suffering is, to use Christian terminology, a sacrifice, a holocaust consumed for the honour of God.

William James quotes Lejeune's *Introduction à la Vie Mystique* in his *Varieties of Religious Experience* (p. 312): 'By poverty he immolates his exterior possessions; by chastity he immolates his body; by obedience he completes the sacrifice, and gives to God all that he yet holds as his own, his two most precious goods, his intellect and his will.' By this sacrifice of the intellect and the will Catholic discipline is completed; that is to say, the devotee turns into a block of wood, a mere mass of burnt coal and cold ashes, and is identified with the Unconscious. And this experience is told by Catholic writers in terms of God, as a sacrifice to him; whereas Zen masters resort to more intellectual or psychological phraseology.

To quote further from Ignatius's *Sayings*: 'I must consider myself as a corpse which has neither intelligence nor will: be like a mass of matter which without resistance lets itself be placed wherever it may please anyone; like a stick in the hand of an old man, who uses it according to his needs and places it where it suits him.' This is the attitude he advises his followers to take towards the Order. The intent of the Catholic discipline is altogether different from that of Zen, and therefore Ignatius's admonition takes on quite a different colouring on the surface. But so far as its psychological experience is concerned, both the Zen masters and the Catholic leaders aim at bringing about the same state of mind, which is no other than realizing the Unconscious in our individual consciousnesses.

The Jesuit Rodriguez gives a very concrete illustration[1] in regard to the virtue of obedience: 'A religious person ought in respect to all the things that he uses to be like a statue which one may drape with clothing, but which feels no grief and makes no resistance when one strips it again. It is in this way that you should feel towards your clothes, your books, your cell and everything else that you make use of. . . .' For your clothes, your books, etc., substitute your griefs, worries, joys, aspirations, etc., which are your psychological possessions just as much as are your physical goods. Avoid using these psychological possessions as if they were your private property, and you are Buddhists living in the Unconscious or with the Unconscious.

Some may say that physical goods are not the same as psychological functions, that without the latter there is no mind and without a mind no sentient being. But I say, without these physical possessions which you are supposed to be in need of, where is your body? Without the body, where is the mind? After all, these psychological

[1] James, pp. 315–16.

functions do not belong to you to the same extent as your clothes, your table, your family, your body, etc., belong to you. You are always controlled by them, instead of your controlling them. You are not master even of your own body which seems to be most intimate to you. You are subject to birth and death. With the body your mind is most closely connected, and this seems to be still more out of your control. Are you not throughout your life a mere plaything of all your sensations, emotions, imaginations, ambitions, passions, etc.?

When Hui-neng and other Zen masters speak of the Unconscious, they may appear to be advising us to turn into cold dead ashes with no mentality, with no feelings, with no inner mechanism commonly associated with humanity, to turn into mere nothingness, absolute emptiness; but in truth this is the advice given by all religionists, this is the final goal all religious discipline aspires to reach. Apart from their theological or philosophical interpretations, to my mind Christians and Buddhists refer to the same fact of experience when they talk about sacrifice and obedience. A state of absolute passivity dynamically interpreted, if such is possible, is the basis of the Zen experience.

The Unconscious is to let 'thy will be done', and not to assert my own. All the doings and happenings, including thoughts and feelings, which I have or which come to me are of the divine will as long as there are on my part no clingings, no hankerings, and 'my mind is wholly disconnected with things of the past, present, and future' in the way described above. This is again the spirit of Christ when he utters: 'Take therefore no thought for the morrow: for the morrow shall take thought for the things of itself. Sufficient unto the day is the evil thereof.' Replace 'the morrow' with 'the future' and 'the day' with 'the present', and what Christ says is exactly what the Zen master would say, though in a more philosophical manner. 'The day' would not mean for the Zen master a period of twenty-four hours as popularly reckoned, but an instant or a thought which passes even before one utters the word. The Unconscious reflects on its surface all such thought-instants, which pass with the utmost rapidity while it itself remains serene and undisturbed. These passing thoughts constitute my consciousness, and in so far as the latter is regarded as belonging to me it has no connection with the Unconscious, and there are attachments, hankerings, worries, disappointments, and all kinds of 'evil thereof'. When they are, however, connected with the Unconscious, they fall away from my consciousness; they cease to be evils, and I share the serenity of the Unconscious. This is, I may say, a phase of absolute passivity.

The conception of the Unconscious leads to many wrong interpretations when it is taken as pointing to the existence of an entity to be designated 'the Unconscious'. Zen masters do not assume such an entity behind our empirical consciousness. Indeed, they are always against assumptions of this nature; they aim at destroying them by all possible means. The Chinese *wu-hsin*, 'without mind', and *wu-nien*, 'without thought' or 'no-thought', mean both the Unconscious and being unconscious. This being so, I sometimes find myself at a loss to present the exact meaning of the Chinese writers whose translations are given in this Essay. The Chinese sentences are very loosely strung together, and each component character is not at all flexible. While read in the original, the sense seems to be clear enough, but when it is to be presented in translation more precision is required to comply with the construction of the language used, in our case English. To do this, much violence is to be practised on the genius of the original Chinese, and instead of a translation it is necessary to have an exposition, or an interpretation, or a paraphrasing; and, as a consequence, the continuous thread of thought woven around the original Chinese characters, with all their grammatical and structural peculiarities, is broken. What we may call the artistic effect of the original is inevitably lost.

In the following dialogue quoted from Hui-chung's sermons[1], arguments are developed around the ideas *wu-hsin* ('no-mind'=unconscious), *yung-hsin* ('using the mind'=conscious striving), *yu-hsin* ('to have a mind'= being conscious), *wu* (as an independent privative particle, 'not', as a prefix, 'dis-', 'un-', etc., as a noun, 'nothingness' or 'no-ness', or 'non-entity'), and *ch'eng-fo* ('attaining Buddhahood', 'becoming a Buddha'). Hui-chung was one of the disciples of Hui-neng, and naturally was anxious to develop the doctrine of *wu-hsin* which means *wu-nien*, the term principally used by Hui-neng, his master. The dialogue opens with the question by Ling-chiao, one of his new followers:

Q. 'I have left my home to become a monk, and my aspiration is to attain Buddhahood. How should I use my mind?'[2]

A. 'Buddhahood is attained when there is no mind which is to be used for the task.'[3]

Q. 'When there is no mind to be used for the task, who can ever attain Buddhahood?'

A. 'By no-mind the task is accomplished by itself. Buddha, too, has no mind.'[4]

[1] *Transmission of the Lamp* (Kokyoshoin edition), fas. 28, fol. 103-4.
[2] *Yung-hsin*, 'to use mind'—that is, 'to apply the mind', 'to train oneself in'.
[3] So long as there are conscious strivings to accomplish a task, the very consciousness works against it, and no task is accomplished. It is only when all the traces of this consciousness are wiped out that Buddhahood is attained.
[4] The idea is that when every effort is put forward to achieve some task, and you are finally exhausted and have come to an end of your energy, you give yourself up so far as your consciousness is concerned. In fact, however, your unconscious mind is still intensely bent on the work, and before you realize it you find the work accomplished. 'Man's extremity is God's opportunity.' This is really what is meant by 'to accomplish the task by no-mind'. But there is also a philosophical

Q. 'The Buddha has wonderful ways and knows how to deliver all beings. If he had no mind, who would ever deliver all beings?'[1]

A. 'To have no mind means to deliver all beings. If he sees any being who is to be delivered he has a mind (*yu-hsin*) and is surely subject to birth and death.'[2]

Q. 'No-mind-ness (*wu-hsin*) is then already here, and how was it that Śākyamuni appeared in the world and left behind ever so many sermons? Is this a fiction?'

A. 'With all the teachings left by him, the Buddha is *wu-hsin* (no-mind, unconscious).'[3]

Q. 'If all his teachings come from his no-mind-ness, they must be also no-teachings.'

A. 'To preach is not (to preach), and not (to preach) is to preach. (All the activities of the Buddha come from no-ness, i.e. Śūnyatā, Emptiness.)'

construction of the idea of Buddha's having no-mind. For, according to Zen philosophy, we are all endowed with the Buddha-nature from which Prajñā issues, illumining all our activities, mental and physical. The Buddha-nature does this in the same way as the sun radiates heat and light, or as the mirror reflects everything coming before it, that is to say, unconsciously, with 'no-mind', *wu-hsin* (in its adverbial sense). Hence it is declared that *fo wu hsin*, 'Buddha is unconscious', or 'By Buddhahood is meant the unconscious'. Philosophically speaking, therefore, no special conscious strivings are necessary; in fact they are a hindrance to the attainment of Buddhahood. We are already Buddhas. To talk about any sort of attainment is a desecration, and logically a tautology. 'Having no-mind', or 'cherishing the unconscious', therefore, means to be free from all these artificial, self-created, double-roofing efforts. Even this 'having', this 'cherishing', goes against *wu-hsin*.

[1] Philosophically stated, how could the Unconscious achieve anything? How would it ever take up the great religious work of carrying all being over to the other shore of Nirvāṇa?

[2] There are two planes of living: the one is the plane of consciousness (*yu-hsin*), and the other is that of unconsciousness (*wu-hsin*). Activities belonging to the first plane with a *yu-hsin* are governed by the laws of karma, while those of the second plane are of the Unconscious, of non-discriminating Prajñā, and characterized with purposelessness and therefore meritlessness. The genuinely religious life takes its start from here, and bears its fruit on the plane of consciousness.

[3] That is, the Buddha with all his worldly activities among us lives on the plane of unconsciousness, in a world of effortlessness and meritlessness, where no teleological categories are applicable.

Q. 'If his teachings come out of his no-mind-ness, is my working karma the outcome of cherishing the idea of a mind (*yu-hsin*)?'

A. 'In no-mind-ness there is no karma. But (as long as you refer to working out your karma) karma is already here, and your mind is subjected to birth and death. How then can there be no-mind-ness (in you)?'

Q. 'If no-mind-ness means Buddhahood, has your Reverence already attained Buddhahood, or not?'

A. 'When mind is not (*wu*), who talks about attaining Buddhahood? To think that there is something called Buddhahood which is to be attained, this is cherishing the idea of a mind (*yu-hsin*); to cherish the idea of a mind is an attempt to accomplish something that flows out (*yu-lou =āsvara* in Sanskrit); this being so, there is no no-mind-ness here.'

Q. 'If there is no Buddhahood to be attained, has your Reverence the Buddha-function?'[1]

A. 'Where mind itself is not, whence is its functioning?'[2]

Q. 'One is then lost in outer no-ness (*wu*); may this not be an absolutely nihilistic view?'

A. 'From the first there is (no viewer and) no viewing; and who says this to be nihilist?'

Q. 'To say that from the first nothing is, is this not falling into emptiness?'

A. 'Even emptiness is not, and where is the falling?'

---

[1] As I stated elsewhere, Buddhist philosophy makes use of two conceptions, Body and Use, in explaining reality. The two are inseparable; where there is any functioning there must be a Body behind it, and where there is a Body its Use will inevitably be recognized. But when it is declared that there is no Buddhahood, how can there be any functioning of it. How then can a Zen abbot have anything to do with Buddhism?

[2] All starts from the Unconscious, all is in the Unconscious, and all sinks down into the Unconscious. There is no Buddhahood, hence no functioning of it. If a thought is awakened and any form of functioning is recognized, there is a discrimination, an attachment, a deviation from the path of the Unconscious. The master stands firmly in the Unconscious and refuses to be transferred to the plane of consciousness. This puzzles the novitiate monk.

Q. 'Both subject and object are negated (*wu*). Suppose a man were all of a sudden to make his appearance here and cut your head off with a sword. Is this to be considered real (*yu*) or not real (*wu*)?'

A. 'This is not real.'

Q. 'Pain or no pain?'

A. 'Pain too is not real.'

Q. 'Pain not being real, in what path of existence would you be reborn after death?'

A. 'No death, no birth, and no path.'

Q. 'Having already attained the state of absolute no-ness, one is perfect master of oneself; but how would you use the mind (*yung-hsin*), when hunger and cold assail you?'

A. 'When hungry, I eat, and when cold I put on more clothes.'

Q. 'If you are aware of hunger and cold, you have a mind (*yu-hsin*).'

A. 'I have a question for you: Has the mind you speak of as a mind (*yu-hsin hsin*) a form?'

Q. 'The mind has no form.'

A. 'If you already knew that the mind has no form, that means that from the first the mind is not, and how could you talk about having a mind?'

Q. 'If you should happen to encounter a tiger or a wolf in the mountains, how would you use your mind (*yung-hsin*)?'

A. 'When it is seen, it is as if it were not seen; when it approaches, it is as if it never approached; and the animal (reflects) no-mind-ness. Even a wild animal will not hurt you.'

Q. 'To be as if nothing were happening, to be in no-mind-ness, absolutely independent of all things, what is the name of such a being?'

A. 'Its name is Vajra the Mahāsattva (Vajra the Great Being).'

Q. 'What form has he?'

A. 'From the first he has no form.'

Q. 'Since he has no form, what is that which goes by the name of Vajra the Great Being?'

A. 'It is called Vajra the Great Formless One.'

Q. 'What merits has he?'

A. 'When your thoughts, just one of them, are in correspondence with Vajra, you are able to erase the grave offences which you have committed while going through cycles of birth and death during Kalpas numbering as many as the sands of the Gangā. The merits of this Vajra the Great One are immeasurable; no word of mouth can reckon them, no minds are capable of describing them; even if one lives for ages numbering as many as the sands of the Gangā, and talks about them, one cannot exhaust them.'

Q. 'What is meant by "one being in one thought in correspondence with it"?'

A. 'When one is forgetful of both memory and intelligence, one is in correspondence with it.'[1]

Q. 'When both memory and intelligence are forgotten, who is it that interviews the Buddhas?'

A. 'To forget means no-ness (*wang chi wu*). No-ness means Buddhahood (*wu chi fo*).'

Q. 'To designate no-ness as no-ness is all very well, but why call it the Buddha?'

A. 'No-ness is emptiness, and the Buddha too is emptiness. Therefore, it is said that no-ness means Buddhahood and Buddhahood no-ness.'

Q. 'If there is not an iota of thing, what is it to be named?'

A. 'No name whatever for it.'

---

[1] 'To be forgetful of memory and intelligence' is an odd expression. 'Forgetful', *wang*, is frequently used to express the idea of the unconscious. To forget both memory and intelligence, which constitute the essence of our empirical consciousness, is to return to the Unconscious, not to cherish any thought of a mind, to do away altogether with a *yung-hsin* or *yu-hsin*, which is the state of no-mind-ness. It is the repetition of the idea stated before, that to be back in the Unconscious is to attain Buddhahood.

76

Q. 'Is there anything resembling it?'

A. 'Not a thing resembling it; the world knows no compeer.'

From this dialogue between Hui-chung and his disciple Ling-chiao, quoted at some length, we can have a glimpse into the meaning of such terms as *wu-hsin, wu-nien, wu, kung,* and *wang,* which we frequently meet in Zen literature and which constitute the central idea, negatively expressed, of Zen philosophy. 'No-mind-ness', 'no-thought-ness' (or 'thought-less-ness'), 'no-ness', 'emptiness', and 'forgetting' are uncouth terms in the English language as employed by the Chinese Zen masters. They sound barbarous, and in many respects utterly unintelligible, and this was indeed the case with the Chinese disciple of Hui-chung, who found it extremely difficult to comprehend the meaning of his master. One must really have an experience in order to get into the spirit of the master, and then the understanding will follow by itself. Whatever this is, all these negative terms tend to point to the conception of the Unconscious, not indeed in the psychological sense but in the deepest metaphysical sense. Although they are mere negations they have a positive signification, and therefore they are identified with Buddhahood, Buddha-nature, Self-nature, Self-being, Suchness, Reality, etc.

So long as one stays in the Unconscious there is no awakening of Prajñā. The Body is there, but no Use; and when there is no Use there is no 'seeing into self-nature', and we all return literally to a static quietness of inorganic matter. Hui-neng was very much against this conception of Dhyāna; hence his philosophy of Prajñā and the motto of Zen Buddhism; the 'seeing into self-nature is becoming the Buddha'.

The greatest advance Hui-neng made in the study of Zen is this idea of seeing into one's self-nature or self-being. Before his time the idea was to contemplate on the serenity

77

and purity of it, which tended to quietism or mere tranquillization. This has already been noticed before, and I will give a further passage bearing on the subject, hoping to clarify the meaning of Hui-neng's notion of seeing into self-being.

A monk asked Chih of Yun-chu of the eighth century, 'What is meant by seeing into one's Self-nature and becoming a Buddha?'

CHIH: 'This Nature is from the first pure and undefiled, serene and undisturbed. It belongs to no categories of duality such as being and non-being, pure and defiled, long and short, taking-in and giving-up; the Body remains in its suchness. To have a clear insight into this is to see into one's Self-nature. Self-nature is the Buddha, and the Buddha is Self-nature. Therefore, seeing into one's Self-nature is becoming the Buddha.'

MONK: 'If Self-nature is pure, and belongs to no categories of duality such as being and non-being, etc., where does this seeing take place?'

CHIH: 'There is a seeing, but nothing seen.'

MONK: 'If there is nothing seen, how can we say that there is any seeing at all?'

CHIH: 'In fact there is no trace of seeing.'

MONK: 'In such a seeing, whose seeing is it?'

CHIH: 'There is no seer, either.'

MONK: 'Where do we ultimately come to?'

CHIH: 'Do you know that it is because of erroneous discrimination that one conceives of a being, and hence the separation of subject and object. This is known as a confused view. For in accordance with this view one is involved in complexities and falls into the path of birth and death. Those with a clearer insight are not like this one. Seeing may go on all day, and yet there is nothing seen by them. You may seek for traces of seeing in them, but nothing, either of the Body or of the Use, is discoverable here. The duality of subject and object is gone—which is called the seeing into Self-nature.'

It is evident that this seeing into self-nature is not an ordinary seeing, in which there is a duality of one who sees and that which is seen. Nor is it a special act of seeing, which, ordinarily understood, takes place at a definite moment and in a definite locality. Nevertheless there is the fact of seeing which cannot be gainsaid. How can such a fact take place in this world of dualities? As long as we cling, to use Buddhist terminology, to this way of thinking, we can never comprehend this Zen experience of seeing into self-nature. To understand it one must have the experience, and at the same time there must be a specially constructed logic or dialectic—by whatever name it may be known— to give to the experience a rational or an irrational inter- pretation. The fact comes first, followed by an intellectuali- zation. Chih of Yun-chu has done his best in the above quotation to express his idea of the seeing according to the way of thinking which then prevailed. This expression may fail to satisfy our present logical demand, but that has nothing to do with the fact itself.

To come back to Hui-neng, Prajñā is awakened in self- nature abruptly (*tun*), and this term *tun* not only means 'instantaneously', 'unexpectedly or suddenly', but signifies the idea that the act of awakening which is seeing is not a conscious deed on the part of self-nature. In other words, Prajñā flashes from the Unconscious and yet never leaves it; it remains unconscious of it. This is the sense of saying that 'Seeing is no-seeing, and no-seeing is seeing', and that the Unconscious or self-nature becomes conscious of itself by means of Prajñā, and yet in this consciousness there is no separation of subject and object. Therefore, says Hui-neng, 'One who understands this truth is *wu nien* ("without thought"), *wu-i* ("without memory"), and *wu-chao* ("with- out attachment").' But we must remember that Hui-neng never advocated the doctrine of mere nothingness, or mere doing-nothing-ness, nor assumed an unknown quantity in the solution of life.

This latter type of misunderstanding seems to have been prevalent soon after the death of Hui-neng, or even while he was alive. In a way this misconstruction appeals to many who have no adequate grasp of the meaning of the transcendental nature of self-being (*svabhāva*). In fact, it is the popular conception of a soul. According to Hui-chung, whose long dialogue with one of his disciples, Ling-chiao, has already been quoted, the popular followers of Hui-neng seem to have gone to the extent of revising the contents of the *T'an-ching* to suit their own interpretation of the Master.

To the inquiry of Hui-chung about Zen Buddhism in the south his visitor had this to report: 'There are at present many Zen masters in the south, and according to them there is the Buddha-nature in every one of us, and this nature is what does all the seeing, hearing, and thinking in him. When he moves his legs or hands, it is the Nature which does it in him, and it is conscious of this experience. The body is subject to birth and death, but the Nature escapes from it as the snake comes out of its skin, or as a man leaves his old house.' To this report of the visitor from the south, Hui-chung adds: 'I also know of this class of Buddhist teachers, and have met many of them in my days of pilgrimage. They are like those heretical philosophers in India who hypostatize a soul. This is really to be deplored. For they tamper with the *T'an-ching*, carrying out all kinds of alteration according to their own ideas against the teaching of their revered Master. The result is the destruction of the principle for which we real followers of our Master stand. . . .'

From the point of textual criticism the *T'an-ching* has apparently suffered much at the hands of succeeding compilers, and even the oldest T'ang copy may not be too exact a report of Hui-neng's discourses. But there is no doubt that even the current copy of the *T'an-ching* contains much of Hui-neng's characteristic standpoint, especially his doctrine of Prajñā, as distinguished from his predecessors and his contemporaries.

The conception of a soul-substance is not so subtle a misconstruction of Hui-neng as that of mere nothingness. We can say that these two conceptions of Prajñā or Self-nature are the two great pitfalls into which most Zen followers, and indeed most Buddhists, are liable to fall. Students of Zen have to guard themselves against committing these faults. What leads them to the pitfall is the attempt to substitute an intellectual or conceptual understanding of an experience for the genuine Zen experience itself. This false proceeding is the source of all grave errors.

Let me quote more from the annals of Zen following Hui-neng, to illustrate how easily we go astray in understanding the relation between Self-nature and Prajñā, Body and Use, the Unconscious and consciousness, Emptiness and a world of becoming, the Unattainable and the attainable, Non-abiding Nirvāna and a realm of birth and death, non-discrimination and logic, no-ness and pluralities, etc.

In what follows, the masters are shown trying hard to make their pupils experience something which lies beyond and yet in dualities, as exemplified above. Fundamentally, the Zen experience consists in seeing into the working of Prajñā, from which starts our ordinary world of contradictions.

Shih-kung Hui-tsang of Fu-chou, who was one of the great disciples of Ma-tsu of the T'ang dynasty, wishing to see what understanding of Zen his head monk had, proposed this question: 'Can you take hold of vacant space?' The monk replied: 'Yes, Master.' 'How do you proceed?' was the demand of the master. The monk thereupon, extending his arm, made a grab at empty space. Remarked the master: 'How can you take hold of space that way?' 'How then?' retorted the monk. No sooner was this said than the master grabbed the monk's nose and pulled it hard. The monk cried aloud, saying: 'This is altogether too hard; you will pull it out!' The master concluded: 'In no other way can you take hold of empty space.'

Here we see that the Unconscious is by no means unconscious of itself, and also that Emptiness is quite a concrete substance which can be held in our own hands. In Hui-neng's days this truth was not so graphically, so vividly, demonstrated. When Hui-neng told one of his disciples, who was a devoted student of the *Puṇḍarīka*, not to be 'turned about' by the Sūtra but to make it 'turn about', the master meant all that was evidenced by Shih-kung, but he was still busy fighting over the field with the same weapon which was in the hands of his disciples; that is, on a more or less conceptual ground.

When Buddhists are told that the Buddha comes from no-whence and departs no-whither, or that the Dharmakāya is like empty space and to be found where there is no-mindness (*wu-hsin*), they are at a loss, or they try to snap at empty space, imagining that this may lead them somewhere. But they will never wake up to Prajñā until their nose is twisted hard and tears come from their eyes.

Even when they are told that every being is endowed with the Buddha-nature and that they are Buddhas, even as they are, they keep themselves from Buddha-hood by reason of their own discriminative understanding, which creates an artificial barrier between themselves and Buddha. Hui-neng's whole mission was to break down this barrier; hence his statement: 'From the first not a thing is.' This must have troubled his disciples ever since it came out of the mouth of a supposedly ignorant wood-cutter of Shinchou.

Shih-kung, the aforementioned master, was asked by a monk: 'How should I escape birth and death?' The master said: 'What is the use of escaping it?' Another time the master's answer was: 'This one knows no birth-and death.' From the point of view of the questioner, 'this one' is the problem indeed.

Is 'this one' the Buddha?

Yu-ti asked Tao-t'ing, another disciple of Ma-tsu: 'Who is the Buddha?' The master called out: 'O Yu-ti!' Yu-ti responded: 'Yes, Master!' Whereupon the master said: 'Don't seek him elsewhere.'

Later, a monk carried this story to Yao-shan, who said: 'Alas, he has bound up that fellow too tightly!' 'What does that mean?' said the monk. Yao-shan too called out: 'O monk!' The monk responded: 'Yes, Master!' Shan then demanded: 'What is that?'

'That' again! What is it this time? Is it once more the Buddha? Let us see if another similar quotation helps us to see into the matter.

A monk asked Pai-chang Hui-hai, the founder of the Zen monastery: 'Who is the Buddha?'

CHANG: 'Who are you?'

MONK: 'I am such and such.'

CHANG: 'Do you know this such and such?'

MONK: 'Most certainly!'

CHANG then raised his *hossu* and said: 'Do you see?'

MONK: 'I see.'

The master did not make any further remark.

Why did Pai-chang remain silent? Did the monk understand who the Buddha was? Or did the master give up the monk as a hopeless case? As far as our ordinary human understanding goes, the monk apparently answered the master correctly. Nothing faulty, then, with the monk? But the trouble with Zen is that it always refuses to remain ordinary, though claiming to be ordinary. One day Pai-chang gave this sermon:

'There is one who, though not eating any rice for a long time, yet feels no hunger; there is another who, though eating rice all day, yet does not feel satisfied.'

Are they two separate individuals? Or are they one and the same individual in spite of their acting and feeling differently? Is there no Buddha here?

Shan-shan Chih-chien was another disciple of Ma-tsu. When he was engaged with the whole company of the monastery in gathering wild herbs, Nan-ch'uan, who was among them, picked one and holding it up said: 'This makes a fine offering!' Chih-chien replied at once: 'Yet he won't give a glance at that or at any delicious food.' Nan-ch'uan said: 'That may be so, but unless each of us tastes it once, we are never done.'

'Prajñā must once be awakened in self-nature; for unless this is experienced we shall never have the chance of knowing the Buddha not only in ourselves but in others. But this awakening is no particular deed performed in the realm of empirical consciousness, and for this reason it is like a lunar reflection in the stream; it is neither continuous nor discrete; it is beyond birth and death; even when it is said to be born, it knows no birth; even when it is said to have passed away, it knows no passing away; it is only when no-mind-ness (the Unconscious) is seen that there are discourses never discoursed, that there are acts never acted. . . .'

From these passages I hope we gain a glimpse into some aspects of Zen thought as promulgated by Hui-neng, and also of its development after him. That the seeing into one's self-nature is the attaining of Buddhahood has become since Hui-neng the most fundamental teaching of Zen Buddhism, especially in the Rinzai school of Zen in Japan as well as in China. This seeing stands contrasted to mere reflecting or contemplating on the immaculateness of self-nature or Buddha-nature, but something still remains of the old habit of quietistic contemplation. For in spite of the fact that seeing is an act just as much as moving a hand or a foot, or as the uttering of words, there is not so much of perceptible muscular movement in seeing as in the shaking of hands, or in ejecting sounds out of the throat and the mouth; and this anatomical peculiarity tends to make us regard the act of seeing from the quietistic point of view. The more intellectual type of mind may remain contented with this tendency, but the case is otherwise with strongly practical people.

The development of Zen thought in China until the day of Hui-neng followed more or less the Indian pattern, but after him its course began to run characteristically along the Chinese channel. The intellectual seeing into Self-nature, so deeply cultivated by the Indian mind, now exhibits what may be called the practical demonstration phase of Chinese Zen. In terms of Chinese Buddhist philosophy, we can state that the Use of Prajñā is now more in evidence than the Body of Prajñā.

Kuei-shan Ling-yu once made the following remark: 'Many masters have indeed an insight into Great Body, but they know nothing of Great Use.' Yang-shan, who was one of the chief disciples of Kuei-shan, transmitting this remark to a monk living in a hut at the foot of the mountain, asked: 'What do you think of the master?' The monk said: 'Repeat that, please.' When Yang-shan was about to do so the monk kicked him down to the ground. Yang-shan reported the incident to the master, who gave a hearty laugh.

On another occasion Yang-shan again experienced this kind of kicking from the foot of Chang-sha Ching, a disciple of Nan-ch'uan. When they were enjoying the moonlight one evening, Yang-shan said: 'People are all endowed with this, but they fail to use it.' Chang-shan said: 'You are the one to use it.' Yang: 'But how would you use it?' Chang with no hesitation kicked his fellow-monk to the ground. Upon rising Yang remarked: 'You are indeed like a tiger.'

The act of kicking is really the act of seeing as far as they both come out of self-nature and reflect it. When this identity is once recognized, the acting achieves an endless development; there is not only kicking, but beating, slapping, pushing down, uttering a cry, etc., as are recorded in Zen literature. Ma-tsu and Shih-tou, both disciples of of Hui-neng, may be regarded as the originators of the dynamic school of Zen, great agents of Use. The following cases may seem to be out of the ordinary in more than one sense, approaching indeed the actions of a lunatic; but from the point of view of 'Great Use', of which the seeing is also one of the practical applications, dancing or the performance of an acrobatic trick may yield a weighty significance.

When P'an-chan Pao-chi, a disciple of Ma-tsu, was about to pass away, he asked: 'Is there anyone among you who will produce my likeness?' Each tried to do his best in sketching the master's portrait, but none pleased him. All were sent away. P'u-hua, one of his own disciples, came out and said: 'I can make your likeness.' 'If so,' said the master, 'why not present it to me?' P'u-hua performed a somersault as he went out of the room. P'an-shan's remark was: 'This fellow, when he goes out in the world as a teacher, will act like a lunatic.'

This prophecy proved true of the life of P'u-hua, as is told in the biography of Lin-chi (Rinzai). When he was invited to dinner with Lin-chi at the house of one of their followers, Lin-chi remarked: 'It is stated that a single hair swallows up a great ocean and a mustard seed holds Mount Sumeru. Is this a miraculous occurrence, or is it naturally so?' P'u-hua overturned the table with his foot. Lin-chi said: 'How rude!' P'u-hua protested: 'Do you know where we are? Rude or refined, this is no place for you to make such a remark.'

The following day there was another occasion for them to be treated to dinner together. Asked Lin-chi: 'How is today's dinner compared with yesterday's?' P'u-hua again turned over the table, at which Lin-chi remarked: 'That

is all right, but all the same you are very ill-mannered.'
P'u-hua retorted : 'What a blind fellow you are! Don't you
know that there is no room in Buddhism for such remarks
as yours on manners?'

Te-shan, a contemporary of Lin-chi, was famous for
this statement : 'Whether you can say a word or not, you
get thirty blows just the same.' Lin-chi told Lo-p'u, one
of his own disciples, to go and interview Te-shan, and
Lin-chi gave him this instruction : 'You ask why one gets
thirty blows even when one can say a word. When Te-shan
strikes you, take hold of his stick and push him out with it.
See how he will behave then.' Everything went as planned
with Te-shan. When pushed with the stick, however, he
quietly walked back to his own quarters. This was reported
to Lin-chi, whose remark was : 'I had some doubt about
him until now, but do you, Lo-p'u, understand him?'
Lo-p'u showed some hesitation, whereupon Lin-chi struck
him.

Chung-i Hung-en, a disciple of Ma-tsu, was once asked by
Yang-shan: 'How can one see into one's self-nature?'
Chung-i said : 'It is like a cage with six windows, and
there is in it a monkey. When someone calls at the east
window, "O monkey, O monkey !" he answers. At the other
windows the same response is obtained.' Yang-shan thanked
him for the instruction, and said : 'Your instructive simile
is quite intelligible, but there is one thing on which I wish
to be enlightened. If the inside monkey is asleep, tired out,
what happens when the outside one comes to interview it?'
Chung-i got down from his straw seat and taking Yang-
shan's arm began to dance, saying : 'O monkey, O monkey,
my interview with you is finished. It is like an animalcule
making its nest among the eyebrows of a mosquito : it
comes out at the street crossing and makes a loud cry :
"Wide is the land, few are the people, and one rarely meets
friends !" '

Chien-nin of Chen-chou was another disciple of Ma-tsu.

He always worked for the Brotherhood. When meal-time came, he carried the rice-holder himself to the dining-room and performed a dance at the entrance, announcing aloud: 'O Bodhisattvas, come and eat your rice!' He then clapped the hands and gave a hearty laugh. This is said to have continued for twenty years. Later, a monk asked Chang-ching: 'What was the ancient master's idea when he danced, clapping his hands?' Ching said: 'It looks as if he were singing praises.' Still later, another monk asked Tai-kuang: 'When Chang-ching refers to giving praises, to whom are the praises given?' Tai-kuang stood up and danced. Thereupon the monk made bows. Kuang remarked: 'What is the meaning of your bows?' It was the monk this time who stood up and danced. Kuang said: 'O you ghost of a wild fox!'

Is this the way to see into one's self-nature? Is this the way Prajñā 'uses' itself? It is remarkable to notice that even at the time of Hui-neng this method of demonstrating the 'Use' of Prajñā was not known among his followers. The most they would do was probably to tell the novices that the Buddha-nature was the Absolute and that when one's idea of birth and death no more obtained it would manifest of its own accord; or that the twinkling of an eye, the raising of the eyebrows, sneezing, etc., all belonged to the Buddha-dharma; or that there was no use trying to see into one's own Nature, because one was of this Nature from the first, and whatever one did came out of it. Dynamic demonstrations, as we may call the later development of Zen thought, were not yet thought of before Ma-tsu and Shih-tou. That they actually developed and constitute the essential characteristic of Zen is one of the most remarkable incidents in the history of religious culture in the Far East.

Whatever we may say of these dynamic demonstrations, there is another striking fact in Zen. It is that the methods resorted to by the Zen masters in order to establish the truth of Zen, or to open the eye of the inquirer, are so varied, so original, so entirely unconventional, that each time we come across them we feel thoroughly refreshed, and frequently as if resurrected from the grave. To see how, after the dam was removed by Hui-neng, the waters of Zen have sought their ever-flowing course, let us cite some of the Zen ways of taking hold of life at its root. In the following the questions take various forms. They are sometimes about Tao, sometimes about the Buddha-nature, sometimes about the meaning of Bodhi-Dharma's coming to China, sometimes about the essence of Buddhism, and so on. However varied the subjects are, they all point to the secret movements of Prajñā, the understanding of which is seeing into one's self-nature, the object of Zen discipline. The quotations below are arranged somewhat irregularly, but they occurred over a period of about one hundred years after Ma-tsu, including his own time.

1. A monk asked Ma-tsu: 'What was the mind of Bodhi-Dharma when he came here from the West?' Ma-tsu asked the monk: 'What is your mind this moment?'

2. P'ang, the noted lay-disciple of Ma-tsu, asked: 'How does water with no muscles and bones support a boat weighing 10,000 tons?' Ma-tsu answered: 'Here is neither water nor a boat, and what muscles and bones are you talking about?'

3. Pai-chang asked: 'What is the ultimate end of Buddhism?' Ma-tsu said: 'This is just where you give up your life.'

4. When Pai-chang was asked by Ma-tsu what way he would use in the demonstration of Zen thought, Pai-chang held up his *hossu*. Ma-tsu asked: 'Is that all? Anything further?' Thereupon Pai-chang threw the *hossu* down.

5. A monk asked Ma-tsu regarding Bodhi-Dharma's idea of coming over to China from the West. The master, striking the monk, said: 'If I do not strike you, all the masters will laugh at me.'

6. Tsung-yin of San-chiao Shan one day gave this sermon: 'If we are to discuss this matter, even the raising of the eyebrows puts us out of the way.' Ma-ku at once asked: 'We don't talk about the raising of the eyebrows; what do you mean by "this matter"?' Tsung-yin said: 'There, you are already out of the way!' Ma-ku upset the master's chair, and the master struck him. Ma-ku had nothing further to say.'

7. A monk asked Pao-yun, of Lu-tsu Shan: 'What is meant by "speaking is no-speaking"?' The master said: 'Where is your mouth?' 'I have no mouth.' 'If so, how do you eat your rice?' To this the monk made no reply. Later, Tang-shan commented: 'That fellow is never hungry, does not want any rice.'

8. While Chang-hsing of Le-tan was found sitting cross-legged facing the wall, Nan-chuan came up and stroked his back. Chan-hsing said: 'Who are you?' 'I am P'u-yuan' (which was Nan-chuan's personal name). 'How are you?' asked Chang-hsing. To this, 'As usual,' was the reply. Said Chang-hsing: 'What a busy life you lead then!'

9. A monk asked Pao-chi, of Pan-shan: 'What is the Toa?'

MASTER: 'Come on.'

MONK: 'I am not yet able to grasp the meaning.'

MASTER: 'Go out.'

10. When Pao-che of Ma-ku Shan one day accompanied his master, Ma-tsu, in his walk, he asked: 'What is Great Nirvāṇa?' The master said: 'Hasten!' 'What is to be hastened, O master?' 'Look at the stream!' was the answer.

11. A Buddhist scholar called on Yen-kuan Ch'i-an, who asked: 'What is your special branch of study?'

SCHOLAR: 'I discourse on the *Avataṁsaka Sūtra*.'

MASTER: 'How many Dharmadhātus does it teach?'

SCHOLAR: 'From the broadest point of view, there are innumerable Dharmadhātus related to one another in the closest possible relationship; but summarily stated, four are reckoned.'

The master then held up his *hossu*, saying, 'To which of those Dharmadhātus does this belong?'

The scholar meditated for a while, trying to find the right answer. The master was impatient and gave out this statement: 'Deliberate thinking and discursive understanding amount to nothing; they belong to the household of ghosts; they are like a lamp in the broad daylight; nothing shines out of them.'

12. A monk asked Tai-mei about Bhodi-Dharma's coming from the West to China, and the master answered: 'No idea whatever in this.' Ch'i-an, learning of this remark, said: 'Two corpses in one coffin.'

13. A monk asked Ling-mo of Wu-hsieh Shan: 'What is the beginning and end of this affair?'

LING-MO: 'Tell me how long this present moment has gone on?'

MONK: 'I am unable to follow you.'

LING-MO: 'I have no room here to cherish questions like yours.'

MONK: 'But you must know some means to treat persons like yourself.'

LING-MO: 'When they come and ask of my treatment, I deal it out to them.'

MONK: 'I then beg of you for treatment.'

LING-MO: 'Is anything lacking with you?'

14. A monk asked Wei-kuan of Hsing-shan Ssu:' What is Tao?'

WEI-KUAN: 'What a fine mountain!'

MONK: 'I am asking you about Tao, so why do you talk about the mountain?'

WEI-KUAN: 'As long as you only know about the mountain there is no chance for you to attain Tao.'

15. Another monk asked Wei-kuan: 'Where is Tao?'

KUAN: 'Right before us.'

MONK: 'Why don't I see it?'

KUAN: 'Because of your egoism you cannot see it.'

MONK: 'If I cannot see it because of my egoism, does your Reverence see it?'

KUAN: 'As long as there is "I and thou", this complicates the situation and there is no seeing Tao.'

MONK: 'When there is neither "I" nor "thou" is it seen?'

KUAN: 'When there is neither "I" nor "thou", who is here to see it?'

16. When Chih-chang of Kuei-sung Ssu had tea with Nan-chuan P'u-yuan, Nan-chuan said: 'We have been good friends, talked about many things and weighed them carefully, and we know where we are now that we each go our own way, what would you say when someone comes up and asks you about ultimate things?'

CHIH-CHANG: 'This ground where we sit now is a fine site for a hut.'

NAN-CHUAN: 'Let your hut alone; how about ultimate things?'

Chih-chang took the tea-set away, and rose from his seat. Whereupon Nan-chuan said: 'You have finished your tea, but I have not.'

CHIH-CHANG: 'The fellow who talks like that cannot consume even a drop of water.'

17. Chih-chang one day came to the Hall and announced: 'I am now going to discourse on Zen. All come up to me.' When the monks came up, the master said: 'When you have listened to the deeds of Kwannon you are able to behave properly in accordance with circumstances.' The monks asked: 'What are the deeds of Kwannon?' The master then snapped his fingers and said: 'Do you all hear that?' The monks said: 'Yes, we hear.' 'This nonsensical company of yours, what do you want to get by coming here?' So saying, the master drove them out of the Hall with a stick, and himself, laughing heartily, returned to the abbot's quarters.

18 (*a*). A monk asked Li-shan: 'All things return to Emptiness, but where does Emptiness return?'

LI-SHAN: 'The mouth is unable to locate it.'

MONK: 'Why not?'

LI-SHAN: 'Because of the oneness of inside and outside.'

(*b*) On another occasion a monk asked: 'What is the idea of Dharma's coming over here from the West?'

LI-SHAN: 'There is no "what" here.'

MONK: 'What is the reason?'

LI-SHAN: 'Just because things are such as they are.'

These two propositions given by Li-shan may be considered commentaries upon one and the same subject; that is, Emptiness and Suchness.

19. Pai-ling one day met P'ang, the lay-Buddhist, in the street. Pai-ling said: 'Have you had occasion to hold up to anyone the truth which you in olden days experienced at Nan-yueh?'

P'ANG: 'Yes, I have.'

PAI-LING: 'To whom?'

P'ANG, pointing to himself, said: 'To this old man.'

PAI-LING: 'Even the praise of Mañjuśrī and Subhūti fails to do justice to you.'

P'ANG now asked: 'Is there anyone who knows of the truth you have experienced?' Pai-ling put on his bamboo hat and went off. P'ang said: 'Good-bye, old man, take good care of yourself.' But Ling walked straight on without looking back.

20. Tan-hsia T'ien-jan, who was a disciple of Shih-tou, one day called on Hui-chung the National Teacher, and asked the attendant if the master was to be seen. The attendant said, 'The master is at home but is not to be seen by visitors.'

TAN-HSIA: 'How unfathomably deep!'

ATTENDANT: 'Even the Buddha's eye is unable to penetrate the depths.'

TAN-HSIA: 'Indeed, the dragon's son is a dragon, the phœnix's is a phœnix.'

Chung the National Teacher having waked from a siesta, the attendant told him about the visitor. Chung gave him twenty blows and chased him out of the house. When Tan-hsia later learned this he said, 'Chung is truly the National Teacher'; and on the following day he called on him again. As soon as he came in his presence, Tan-hsia spread out his cushion to perform his bowing. But Chung the Teacher said: 'Not necessary, not necessary.' When Tan-hsia stepped backward, Chung said: 'That's right.' Tan-hsia then walked around the master and left. Chung's conclusion was: 'Being far away from the time of the old masters, people are neglectful of what they ought to do. Even in thirty years from now such a fellow as this one is rarely met.'

21. When Hui-lang of Chao-t'i saw Ma-tsu, the latter asked: 'What do you seek here?'

HUI-LANG: 'I am after the insight attained by the Buddha.'

MA-TSU: 'The Buddha has no such insight; such belongs to Evil Ones. You say you come from Nan-yueh, but you seem not to have seen Shih-tou yet. You had better go back to him.'

Hui-lang accordingly went back to Nan-yueh and asked: 'What is the Buddha?'

SHIH-TOU: 'You have no Buddha-nature.'

HUI-LANG: 'How about those natures moving about us?'

SHIH-TOU: 'They have it.'

HUI-LANG: 'Why then not I?'

SHIH-TOU: 'Because you fail to see to it yourself.'

This is said to have opened his eye to his self-nature. Afterwards he lived at Cho-t'i and whatever monks came to him for instruction were sent away with: 'Begone! you have no Buddha-nature!'

To help understand this treatment of Hui-lang, let me append two more such cases from the Chuan-teng Lu.

Chang-ching Hui-yun was once asked by a monk: 'What is that which is called the Buddha-nature in this body of the Four Elements and the Five Skandhas?' The master called out the monk's name, and the monk answered: 'Yes.' The master remained silent for a while, and then remarked: 'There is no Buddha-nature in you.'

When E-hu Ta-i (735–818) was asked by the Emperor Shun-tsung, 'What is the Buddha-nature?' the master answered: 'It is not far away from where your Majesty's question comes.'

Hui-ch'ao of Shu-shan was once visited by Tung-shan, who asked him for instruction. Hui-ch'ao said: 'You have already found your abode (you are no more a monk on pilgrimage), and what makes you come over here for my instruction?'

Tung-shan: 'I still have an uneasy mind, over which I have no power. That is why I am here specially to see you.'

Hui-ch'ao called out, 'O Liang-chieh' (which was the personal name of Tung-shan). To which Tung-shan replied: 'Yes, Master.'

Hui-ch'ao: 'What is that?'

Tung-shan uttered not a word. Hui-ch'ao gave his verdict: 'A magnificent Buddha, but unfortunately he emits no light.'

PAI-CHANG one day finished a sermon, and seeing the brotherhood about to leave the Hall called out: 'O Brethren!' They all turned back, whereupon the master said: 'What is that?' This remark came to be much talked about among Zen students of the day.

22. Chen-lang came up to Shih-tou and asked: 'What is the idea of Dharma's coming over here from the West?'

SHIH-TOU: 'Ask the post over there.'

CHEN-LANG: 'I do not understand.'

SHIH-TOU: 'Neither do I.'

This remark made Chen-lang realize the truth. Later, when a monk came to him asking for his instructions, he called out: 'O reverend sir!' The monk answered, 'Yes,' whereupon Chen-lang said: 'You are turning away from yourself.' 'If so, why do you not see to it that I behave properly?' This said, Chen-lang wiped his eyes as if trying to see better. The monk had no words.

23. Shih-tou once made this statement: 'Whatever talk you have about it, however you conduct yourself, such things have no concern with it.' Wei-yen of Yao-shan commented: 'Even when you do not talk about it, even when you do not conduct yourself in any way, such things have no concern with it.'

SHIH-TOU: 'Here is no room even for a needle's point.'

WEI-YEN: 'Here it is like planting flowers on a rock.'

24. When Yao-shan Wei-yen was sitting cross-legged quietly, a monk came to him and said: 'In this immovable position what are you thinking?'

YAO-SHAN: 'Thinking of that which is beyond thinking.'

MONK: 'How do you go on with thinking that which is beyond thinking?'

YAO-SHAN: 'By not-thinking.'

25. A monk asked: 'I have a doubt which I wish you to decide.'

YAO-SHAN: 'Wait until I come up to the Hall this evening, when I will have your doubt settled.'

When the Brotherhood assembled in the Hall, the master told the monk to appear before him. The monk walked up to him, when Yao-shan came down from his chair and taking hold of him said: 'O monks, here is one who has a doubt.' So saying, he pushed away from him and returned to his own quarters.

Later, Hsuan-chiao commented: 'Did Yao-shan really settle the doubt the monk had? If this was the case, where was the point? If this was not the case, why did the master tell the monk he would settle it for him at the time of the evening service?'

26. Yang-shan asked Kuei-shan about Bodhi-Dharma's idea of coming over to China from India, and Kuei-shan replied: 'What a fine lantern this is!'

YANG-SHAN: 'Is this not it, and no other?'

KUEI-SHAN: 'What do you mean by "this"?'

YANG-SHAN: 'What a fine lantern this is!'

KUEI-SHAN: 'Sure enough, you do not know.'

Let me remark in passing that in Zen it is often difficult for the uninitiated to know where to locate the intention of the master's statement. For instance, in the present case Kuei-shan's 'You do not know' is not to be understood in its popular sense of ignorance. For here Kuei-shan is not referring to Yang-shan's not knowing Zen; on the contrary, Kuei-shan knows well where Yang-shan stands, and also that Yang-shan understands well where Kuei-shan stands. For this reason we cannot merely follow what they say to each other; we have first to get into the inner side or into the intent of their expressions. A monk asked Yao-shan to enlighten him, as he was still groping in the dark as to the meaning of his own life. Yao-shan kept quiet for a while. This keeping quiet is pregnant with meaning, and if the monk were ready for it he could have comprehended what made Yao-shan remain silent. But in point of fact the monk failed, and Yao-shan continued: 'It is not difficult for me to say a word to you on the matter before us. The point, however, is to grasp the meaning, as soon as it is uttered, without a moment of deliberation. When this is done there is an approach to the truth. On the other hand, there is a delay on your part, and you begin to reason things out, and the fault will be finally laid at my door. It is after all better to keep the mouth closed so that we both escape further complications.' This statement by Yao-shan is quite to the point. Words appeal to our discursive understanding and lead to ratiocination, while Zen's course is in the other direction, pointing to the time before words are uttered.

27. A monk came to Shih-lou, a disciple of Shih-tou, and asked: 'I am still ignorant of my original birth. Will you kindly find some means to enlighten me?'

SHIH-LOU: 'I have no ears.'

MONK: 'I know that I was at fault.'

SHIH-LOU: 'Oh no, it is my own fault.'

MONK: 'Where is your fault, O Master?'

SHIN-LOU: 'The fault is where you say you are at fault.'

The monk made bows, and the master struck him.

28. Hua-lin was asked by Shih-tou his teacher: 'Are you a Zen monk or an ordinary one?'

HUA-LIN: 'I am a Zen monk.'

SHIH-TOU: 'What is Zen?'

HUA-LIN: 'Raising the eyebrows, moving the eyes.'

SHIH-TOU: 'Bring your original form forward and let me see; I have no use for the raising of the eyebrows or the moving of the eyes.'

HUA-LIN: 'O Master, do away with your raising the eyebrows, and moving the eyes, and see me where I am.'

SHIH-TOU: 'They are done away with.'

HUA-LIN: 'The presentation is over.'

29. Ts'ui-wei Wu-hsiao was one day taking a walk inside

the Dharma-hall, when T'ou-tzu approached and making bows respectfully asked: 'O Master, how do you instruct us regarding the secret message brought by Bodhi-Dharma from the West?' Ts'ui-wei stopped walking for a while. T'ou-tzu asked for instruction again, whereupon the master said: 'What, do you want a second dipperful of slop?' Tou-tzu bowed and retreated. The master's parting words were: 'Don't be neglectful of it'; and T'ou-tzu's response was: 'When time comes, it will strike root and a young plant will grow.'

30. When Ts'ui-wei was placing offerings before the Arhats, a monk asked: 'Tan-hsia' (who was Ts'ui-wei's teacher), 'put the wooden Buddhas into a fire, and how is it that you make offerings to the Arhats?' The master answered: 'Even when put into a fire, they never burn; as to my making offerings to the Arhats, just let me alone.'

Another time a monk asked: 'When you make offerings to the Arhats, do they come to receive them, or not?' Retorted the master: 'Do you eat every day?' The monk remained silent, and the master finished thus: 'Few are intelligent ones.'

31. When Tao-wu Yuan-chih and Yun-yen were in attendance upon their teacher Yao-shan, the latter said: 'Where the intellect is at its end, beware of uttering a word. If you do, horns will grow on you. What do you say to this, Brother Chih?' Yuan-chih then left the room. Yun-yen asked Yao-shan: 'Why did not my Brother Chih answer your question?' Said Yao-shan: 'My back aches today; Brother Chih knows it well. You go to him and ask.' Thereupon, Yun-yen went out and, seeing Chih, said to him: 'How was it that a while ago you failed to answer the master?' Chih, however, told him to go back to the master, for the master knew it all.

32. Te-ch'ien of Hua-ting was popularly known as a ferryman, for he lived in a little boat on the Wu-chiang. One day a monk called Chan-hui, who was advised by a

friend of his to see this boatman, came specially to pay him respect. The boatman asked: 'At what monastery do you stay?'

SHAN-HUI: 'I stay at no monastery. The place I stay at no one knows.'

BOATMAN: 'What does it look like, the place that no one knows?'

SHAN-HUI: 'As far as our sight extends, I see nothing comparable to it.'

BOATMAN: 'Where did you learn to say that?'

SHAN-HUI: 'It is beyond the reach of ears and eyes.'

The boatman laughed heartily, saying: 'However fine your philosophy is, it serves you no better than the post to which your donkey is tied. When a line one thousand feet long is dropped into the pool, the intent is to sound the very depths of the abyss. Don't bite at the bait, but speak out quick, quick!' When Shan-hui was about to open his mouth, the boatman with his pole pushed him into the water, which made Shan-hui abruptly realize *satori*. As to the boatman, he immediately left the boat, and nobody knew where he finished the remainder of his life.

33. When Kao the Sha-mi called one rainy day on Yao-shan, the master said: 'So you are come.'

KAO: 'Yes, Master.'

YAO: 'You are very wet, are you not?'

KAO: 'No beating of such a drum.'

Yun-yen and T'ao-wu happened to be with Yao-shan, and Yun said: 'No hide is here, and what drum is to be beaten?' Tao said: 'No drum is here, and what hide is to be beaten?' Yao-shan finally said: 'What a fine tune we have today!'

34. When meal-time came, Yao-shan himself beat the drum and Kao the Sha-mi came dancing into the dining-room with his bowl. Seeing this, Yao-shan put down the drumsticks and said: 'What tune is that?'

KAO: 'Tune Number 2.'

YAO: 'What is tune Number 1?'

KAO filled his bowl with rice from the vessel and went away.

From these 'questions and answers' which were exchanged between Zen students during the one hundred and fifty years after the passing of Hui-neng, the reader can gauge the extent of development effected by Zen thought. The scene has almost entirely changed from that which was visible until the time of the Sixth Patriarch. Only what may be called Sūtra terminology had been in use in the exposition of Zen. No one had ever thought that beating, kicking, and other rough methods of treatment would be accorded to the students. 'Mere seeing' is gone, and acting has taken its place. Has that materially changed in any way the spirit of Zen in its transmission from Bodhi-Dharma down to the Sixth Patriarch? Outwardly yes, but in spirit no. For there is a constant flow of the same thought underlying all those 'questions and answers'. What has undergone change is the method used. The spirit is that of Hui-neng, who declares: 'I establish no-thought-ness (*wu-nien* the Unconscious) as the Principle [of my teaching], formlessness as the Body, and abodelessness as the Source.' This declaration is the foundation of Zen teaching, and can be traced in those varied answers given by the masters either in words or gestures.

Wu-nien (no-thought) is psychological, *wu-hsiang* (no-form) ontological, and *wu-chu* (no-abode) is moral. The first and the third have a subjective sense while the second has an objective sense. They all practically and ultimately mean the same thing, but Zen is most interested in psychology, in realizing the Unconscious; in going beyond it, for when this is gained an abode that is no-abode is found, and the mind is altogether detached from form, which also means detachment from the mind itself; and this is a state of *wu-nien*, 'no-thought-ness'. Hitherto this has been studied in connection with Prajñā, because Hui-neng was

intensely occupied with the problem of Prajñā and Dhyāna,
reflecting the spirit of his age. Now, let us see in what light
this no-thought-ness or the Unconscious is to be understood
when it is related to our ethical life.

We now come to the most significant discussion in the
teaching of Zen. As far as the seeing into one's inner being,
known as self-nature, is concerned, the matter is more or
less on the epistemological plane, and does not seem to
affect our practical life from the ethical point of view. But
when Prajñā is considered not from the point of view of
seeing but from the point of view of acting, it goes directly
into the very heart of life. Most of the 'questions and
answers' cited above have been extracted from annals of the
early history of Zen with a view to showing the individual
masters' methods of teaching how to awaken Prajñā in the
minds of the pupils—minds most obstinately warped
because of their dualistic interpretation of life and the
world. In the following examples we will try to see into
the inner working of Prajñā in their daily behaviour.

1. A monk asked Ching-t'sen, of Chang-sha: 'What is
meant by 'one's everyday thought is the Tao'?''
CHING-T'SEN: 'When I feel sleepy, I sleep; when I want
to sit, I sit.'
MONK: 'I fail to follow you.'
CHING-T'SEN: 'In summer we seek a cool place; when
cold we sit by a fire.'
2. A Vināya master called Yuan came to Tai-chu
Hui-hai, and asked: 'When disciplining oneself in the Tao,
is there any special way of doing it?'
HUI-HAI: 'Yes, there is.'
YUAN: 'What is that?'
HUI-HAI: 'When hungry one eats; when tired, one
sleeps.'
YUAN: 'That is what other people do; is their way the
same as yours?'

Hui-hai: 'Not the same.'

Yuan: 'Why not?'

Hui-hai: 'When they eat, they do not just eat, they conjure up all kinds of imagination; when they sleep, they do not just sleep, they are given up to varieties of idle thoughts. That is why theirs is not my way.'

The Vināya master did not further pursue the Zen master.

3. When the entire body of the Brotherhood at Pai-chang was engaged in tilling the farm, there was one monk who, hearing the dinner drum, at once raised his spade and gave out a hearty laugh and went off. Huai-hai the master remarked: 'What an intelligent fellow! This is the way to enter the Kwannon gate of truth.' When he returned to the monastery, he sent for the said monk and asked: 'What was the truth you saw a while ago when you heard the drum?' Answered the monk: 'Nothing much, Master. As I heard the dinner drum go, I went back and had my meal.' This time it was the master who gave out a hearty laugh.

4. When Kuei-shan Ling-yu was sitting in the Hall, the monk-cook beat the *mokugyo* (lit., 'wooden fish') to announce the meal-time. Hearing it, the monk who was attending to the fire set down the poker, and clapping his hands, laughed heartily. The master said: 'Here among my Brotherhood is a man of real intelligence.' Later he sent for the monk and asked: 'What was the matter with you?' The fire-tender replied: 'I had no breakfast this morning, and being so hungry was intensely glad to hear the gong.' The master nodded.

5. Yun-yen asked Pai-chang Huai-hai: 'Reverend Sir, you seem to be busily employed every day; whom is it for?'

Huai-hai: 'There is one man who wants it.'

Yun-yen: 'Why not let him do it himself?'

Huai-hai: 'He keeps no house.'

6. When Huang-po Hsi-yun left Nan-ch'uan, the latter

saw him off as far as the monastery gate. Holding up Yun's travelling hat, Ch'uan said: 'You are enormously big, but your hat is none too big for you, is it?'

YUN replied: 'That may be so, but the entire cosmos is readily covered underneath.'

CH'UAN: 'How about me, then?'

YUN put the hat on and went off.

7. When Yun-chi of Chung-nan Shan was studying Zen under Nan-ch'uan, he asked: 'People do not know where the *māṇi*-jewel is, and yet I am told it is preserved deep down in the Tathāgatagarbha; what is the Garbha?'

NAN-CH'UAN: 'That which walks along with you.'

YUN-CHI: 'What about that which does not walk with me?'

NAN-CH'UAN: 'That is also the Garbha.'

YUN-CHI: 'What then is the *māṇi*-jewel itself?'

NAN-CH'UAN called out: 'O Brother!'

YUN-CHI answered at once: 'Yes, Reverend Sir.'

NAN-CH'UAN: 'Begone, you don't understand my words!'

YUN-CHI, however, thereby found his way into Zen.

WHAT do we gather from all these citations about Zen life? What are the outward expressions or behaviour of the Unconscious?

The most famous saying of Ma-tsu is, 'This mind is the Buddha himself,' which has been in fact one of the main thoughts advocated by all the Zen masters preceding him; but to this Ma-tsu added: 'One's everyday thought (or mind) is the Tao.' In Chinese the same character *hsin* is used for 'thought' as well as for 'mind', and by thought or mind in this case is meant the state of consciousness we have in ordinary circumstances, in our everyday life, when we live like the sun which shines on the just and on the unjust, like the lilies of the field which bloom in their full glory even when not admired. The mind in 'everyday mind (or thought)' has thus no reference to our psychological conception of mind or soul; it is rather a state of mind in which there is no specific consciousness of its own workings, reminding one of what the philosophers call 'transcendental apperception'. This may correspond to what I have called the Unconscious (*wu-hsin* or *wu-nien*) in the preceding sections.

When Ma-tsu and other Zen leaders declare that 'this mind is the Buddha himself', it does not mean that there is a kind of soul lying hidden in the depths of consciousness, but that a state of unconsciousness, psychologically stated, which accompanies every conscious and unconscious act of mind is what constitutes Buddhahood.

Understanding Ma-tsu's statements in this light, the commentaries by Ching-t'sen and Tai-chu became intelligible. 'When I feel sleepy, I sleep; when I want to sit, I sit.' Or: 'When hungry I eat, when tired, I sleep.' Or: 'In summer we seek a cool place, and when cold we sit by a fire.' Are these not our everyday acts, acts done naturally, instinctively, effortlessly, and unconsciously? The hungry monks at Pai-chang and Kuei-shan, too, behaved in the most spontaneous manner. They illustrate in their practical life what all the Zen masters would like to see. So with Hsi-yun, who bade farewell to his friend Huang-po by putting on his travelling bamboo hat, even without looking back. He acted like those hungry monks who, upon hearing the dinner-bell, threw down whatever tools they had and made towards the refectory. It was the same with Yun-chi, who responded 'Yes' to the call of his master Nan-ch'uan. The gong is struck and the air rings with a boom. Is this not our 'everyday life', or, as Ma-tsu and Nan-ch'uan would call it, 'everyday thought'? We are kept busy with one thing or another from morning till evening, and 'whom is it all for?' Says Pai-chang, 'There is someone who wants it,' but where is this fellow, this grand master who seems to be directing all our movements, keeping us very busy, but who does not know the act of 'housekeeping'? He seems to be everywhere, but cannot be located; he is abodeless.

'The Buddha-body fills the Dharmadhātu and manifests itself universally before all beings. It works, it achieves in response to conditions, and yet it never leaves this seat of Bodhi.' This is the general Mahāyāna teaching as promulgated in India. When this 'seat of Bodhi' is located, the abodeless master who makes us keep house for him may be located. Such terms as 'housekeeping', 'living one's everyday life', or 'thinking one's everyday thought' bring Zen intimately into our life. The Unconscious does not seem to lie too deeply in our homely consciousness.

Shan-hui of Chia-shan (805–881), who obtained an insight into the teaching of Zen by being mercilessly pushed into a river by the boatman-master of Hua-ting, had a young attendant who served him sometimes. When Shan-hui came to preside over a monastery, the monk was sent out on a Zen pilgrimage through the country. He visited several masters but did not find much satisfaction with them. In the meantime his own master's fame went out far and wide. He hurriedly came back and asked: 'O Master, when you are such a worker of wonders why did you not teach me long before I was sent away on pilgrimage?' The master said: 'When you were here with me, you wanted to prepare rice, and I started a fire; you set the table, dished out rice, and I got out my bowl. When did I ever behave contrary to your order?' This is said to have enlightened the young disciple. A similar story is told of Ch'ung-hsin, who succeeded Tao-wu.

Te-shan Hsuan-chien (780–865), of Shu, was a great student of the *Diamond Sūtra* before he had his eyes opened to the truth of Zen. As a full-fledged master he was known for his swinging a stick on his students. He is popularly coupled with Lin-chi (Rinzai), who uttered a '*Kwatz!*' over anybody approaching him with a question. Te-shan's famous statement was: 'Thirty blows when you can say a word, thirty blows when you cannot say a word!' 'To say a word' is almost a technical term with Zen, and means anything which is brought forward, whether in words or in gestures, regarding the central fact of Zen. 'Giving a blow' in this case means that all such demonstrations are of no avail whatever. In short, according to Te-shan, Zen is a philosophy of absolute negations which are at the same time absolute affirmations; unless one gains a certain insight into this dialectic of negation-affirmation one has no right to say a word about Zen.

When one evening Te-shan made this declaration, a monk came out from the audience, and was about to make bows before him when the master struck him. The monk protested: 'How is it that you strike me, Master, even before I have proposed a question?' The master asked: 'Where do you come from?' 'I come from Kona.' 'Even before you boarded a boat, you deserved thirty blows,' was his verdict.

Lung-ya asked: 'If I threatened to cut your head off with the sharpest sword one can find in the world, what would you do?'

The master pulled his head in.

Lung-ya said: 'Your head is off!'

The master smiled.

Later, Lung-ya came to Tung-shan and mentioned this episode to him. Tung-shan asked: 'What did Te-shan say?'

LUNG-YA: 'He said nothing.'

TUNG-SHAN: 'Don't say that he said nothing. Show me the head you then cut off.'

Lung-ya acknowledged his fault and apologized.

This story was reported back by someone to Te-shan, who then remarked: 'Old Tung-shan has no judgment. That fellow (Lung-ya) has been dead for some time, and what is the use of trying to save him?'

A monk asked: 'What is Bodhi (enlightenment)?'

The master responded: 'Don't scatter your dirt here!'

A monk asked: 'Who is the Buddha?'

The master said: 'He is an old Bhikshu of the Western country.'

One day Te-shan gave a sermon in which he said: 'When you question, you commit a fault; when you do not, you give offence.' A monk came forward and began to bow, whereupon the master struck him. The monk said: 'I have just begun my bowing, and why do you strike me?' 'If I wait for you to open your mouth, all will be over.'

The master sent his attendant to fetch I-t'sun (i.e. Hsueh-feng). When he came, the master said: 'I have just sent for I-t'sun, and what is the use of *your* coming up?' T'sun made no reply.

109

Seeing a monk approach, Te-shan closed the gate. The monk came up and knocked. The master said: 'Who are you?'

MONK: 'I am a lion.'

The master opened the gate and the monk bowed to the ground. Seeing this, the master got astride his neck and said: 'O beast, why do you keep loitering about here (i.e. in a monastery)?'

Te-shan was ill, and a monk asked: 'Is there one who is not ill?'

'Yes, there is one.'

'Who is this one who is not ill?'

'O Father!' cried the master.

Do we not also here have tidings of 'your everyday thought which is the Tao'? Do we not trace here the working of the Unconscious which responds almost 'instinctively' to the requirements of the occasion?

Let me give another quotation from Pen-hsien (941–1008), who belongs to the Hogen (Fa-yuan) school of Zen. He once said: 'In the study of Buddhism it is not necessary to know much about those Zen interviews which have taken place before us, nor is it necessary to pick out certain striking phrases from the sūtras or from the śastras and regard them as expressing the highest truth. Discussions on such subjects are left to those addicted to intellectualization. Mere cleverness is not meant to cope with the facts of birth and death. If you really wish to get into the truth of Zen, get it while walking, while standing, while sleeping or sitting, while talking or remaining silent, or while engaged in all kinds of your daily work. When you have done this, see whose doctrine you are following, or what sūtras you are studying.'

On another occasion he had this to say: 'We get up early in the morning, wash our hands and faces, clean our mouths, and take tea. Finishing tea, we make bows before the Buddha. The bowing finished, we go to the abbot, to the chief officers of the monastery and pay them our respects. This finished, we go to the refectory, where we dish out gruel for our Brotherhood. This finished, we take our seats and eat breakfast. This finished, we go down to our quarters, where we have our morning sleep. This finished, we get up and wash our hands and faces, and clean our mouths. This finished, we sip tea and attend various affairs. This finished, the meal-time comes, and we go to the dining-room, where dishes are arranged in order, and we take our midday meal. The meal finished, washing is done, and afterwards tea is served. The tea finished, various affairs are attended to. This done, the evening is here, and the evening service is regularly carried on at several places. This finished, we come to the abbot and pay him respect. This finished, it is now the first period of the night, when another service is performed. This finished, we proclaim "good night" to the monks' quarters. This finished, we call on the abbot, and then we do our bowings before the Buddha, read the sūtras, walk reciting, or practise the nembutsu (nien-fo). Besides this, we sometimes go to the villages, to the cities, to the markets, or visit laymen's houses, and so on. This being so, we are on the move all the time, and where is that which you call the immovable, or that which eternally abides in the Samādhi of Nāga? . . .'

In this, Pen-hsien is evidently referring to his routine work going on at the monastery. While he emphasizes the dynamic side of Zen life in contradistinction to the quietism still prevailing in certain quarters of the Buddhist world of his day, the main idea running through this sermon is that of 'your everyday thought', of 'sleeping when tired and eating when hungry', of sipping tea which is offered to you, of responding with 'yes' when called to; that is to say, of following the dictates of the Unconscious.

When Zen is to be grasped in these actions daily performed by every one of us, and given no special thought
because of their sharing the nature of mere reflex action,
is Zen life to be considered as no different from a life of
instincts or a series of impulses? Does the Zen master sub-
scribe to the view that 'those creatures moving about you
have more of the Buddha-nature than yourself', that the
chirping birds or the cat which climbs up the pillar are
worthier friends of the master than those question-asking
monks? Zen almost seems to advocate action. In all
religion there is a constant tendency to regard passivity or
passive activity as the highest expression of its life. 'The fowls
of the air', 'the lilies of the field', and 'the grass of the field'
are given as examples to follow when one is to understand
the thought of God. A great mediaeval theologian is
quoted as saying: 'What I know of the divine sciences and
of holy Scripture I learned in woods and fields, by prayer
and meditation. I have had no other masters than the
beeches and the oaks.' Another great divine declares:
'Listen to a man of experience; thou wilt learn more in the
woods than from books. Trees and stones will teach thee
more than thou canst acquire from the mouth of a magister.'

A kind of naturalism is almost universally recommended by religion, even by Christianity, which lays so
much stress on the moral life as distinct from the life of the
instincts. It is no wonder that its history is littered with
ideas and even practices reflecting those of the Free Spirit.
By virtue of its strong ethical idealism, Christianity has
stood against the occasional attacks of antinomianism and
spiritual lawlessness, but the fact remains that the feeling
of absolute dependence, or letting God take entire possession
of your will and thought, inevitably leads to the libertinism
of natural impulses, which is 'the freedom of the spirit'.

Such statements can be found in most mystical books
whose principal teaching is to get beyond the intellect
and plunge into the abyss of unknowability. When God, to

112

whom no intellectual categories are applicable, such as essence, quality, quantity, relation, situation, space, time, action, and passion; God, unnamed and unnameable, who is 'a perpetual now, the bottomless abyss, the darkness of silence, the desert wilderness'—when this God takes possession of you in such a way that you are lost in God, you glide away into God, then all that you are, all that you do, must be considered altogether inevitable.

Things which rise from the darkness of silence, from the wilderness of the Unconscious, do not belong to the realm of human reflection and deliberation. Hence the mystics are the lilies of the field and the grass of the field as well. They are beyond good and bad. They know no moral responsibilities, which are ascribable only when there is the consciousness of good and bad. If this is the religious life, it is the philosophy of anarchism or nihilism. But the conclusion we can draw from the mystics of the two widely divergent teachings, Christian and Buddhist, for instance, Eckhart, Suso, Tauler, Ruysbroeck, and others on the Christian side, and all the Zen masters quoted everywhere in this book, seems to point alike to this nihilistic smashing of all human moral standards. Is this really so?

To transcend intellectualism does not necessarily mean moral anarchism, but psychologically the one leads to the other, for moral deliberation is impossible without assuming the supremacy of the intellect. When, therefore, the one is denied, the other is apt to recede. One Christian mystic says: 'To affirm God is actually to reduce him. To say that God is good, just, intelligent, is to enclose him within a created conception which is applicable only to created things.'

Another Christian mystic, who is described by the first as not of an orthodox sort, declares that: 'In my essential being I am by nature God. For myself, I neither hope nor love, and I have no faith, no confidence in God. . . . So long as man has a tendency to virtue and desires to do God's very precious will, he is still imperfect, being preoccupied with the acquiring of things. . . . [The perfect man] can never either believe in virtues, or have additional merit, or commit sins. . . .' The one may pronounce the other heretical and immoral, but so far as their dialectic goes, both are sound and referring to the same facts of experience. Chao-chou says, 'I do not like to hear the word Buddha,' or, 'When you pronounce the word Buddha, clean your mouth for three years,' to get rid of the filth you thereby breathe. Zen has something of this anarchistic naturalism in its teaching.

In Bodhi-Dharma's sayings, discovered at Tun-huang, we find this: 'Those Buddhists who discipline themselves in the doctrine of absolute Buddhahood should make their minds like a piece of rock, be darkly ignorant, remain unaware [of all things], have no discrimination, behave unconcernedly with all things, resembling an idiot. And why? Because the Dharma has no awareness, no intelligence; because it gives no fearlessness; it is the final abode of rest. It is like a man who has committed a capital crime deserving decapitation, but who, pardoned by the king, is freed from the worry of death. It is so with all beings. They commit the ten evil deeds and the five grave offences, making them bound surely for hell. But the Dharma, like a king, has the unsurpassable power of pardoning all sins so as to release all offenders from being punished. Here is a man who is friendly with the king. He happens to be somewhere outside his native home and murders men and women. Being captured, he is about to be punished because of his misdeed. He does not know what to do, he is altogether helpless, when he unexpectedly sees his king and thereby he is released. Even when a man violates the precepts, committing murder, adultery, theft, and is terrified at the prospect of falling into hell, he is awakened to the presence of his inner Dharma-king, and thereby effects his emancipation.'

This is almost the teaching of the followers of the Free Spirit. The Dharma-king is here their God. Another quotation from another Tung-huang document belonging to the Zen sect reads:

Q. 'I am afraid of hell, I want to confess [all my sins], and discipline myself in the Tao.'

A. 'Where is this "I"? What does it look like?'

Q. 'I know not where!'

A. 'If you do not know where your "I" is, who is it that falls into hell? If you do not know what it looks like, this is no less than an illusively conceived existence. Just because of this illusion, there is hell for you.'

Q. 'If the Tao itself is an illusion, how is this illusion formed?'

A. 'The Dharma has no magnitude, no form, no altitude. To illustrate: here is a big stone in the court attached to your house. You sit on it, sleep on it, and have no feeling of fear. One day you suddenly conceive the idea of painting a picture on it. You hire an artist and have a Buddha's figure painted on it and you take it for the Buddha. No longer dare you sleep on it, you are fearful of desecrating the image, which was originally nothing but a huge rock. It is due to the change in your mind that you no more sleep on it. And what is this so-called mind, too? It is but your own brush pieced out of your imagination, which has turned the stone into the Buddha-figure. The feeling of fear is your own creation; the stone itself is indeed devoid both of merit and demerit.

'All is mind-made. It is like a man's painting a devil, a creature from hell, or a dragon, or a tiger. He paints it, looks at it, and is frightened. There is, however, nothing at all in the painted figure itself which is fearsome. All is the brushwork of your own imagination, your own discrimination. From the first, not a thing there is, except what you have made out of your own illusive mind.'

When 'I' is an illusion, all that goes on in the name of

this agent must be an illusion too, including moral sins, various kinds of feelings and desires, and hell and the land of bliss. With the removal of this illusion, the world with all its multiplicities will disappear, and if there is anything left which can act, this one will act with utmost freedom, with fearlessness, like the Dharma-king himself, indeed as the One. But at the same time the possibility of a moral world is annulled, and then how can licentiousness be distinguished from holiness? Or is there no such thing as licentiousness or criminality or moral evil in a world of no illusions?

Whether we start from the doctrine of union or from that of illusion, the mystics, Buddhist and Christian, both seem to find their practical conclusion in the conception of moral irresponsibility, in whatever way this may be understood. So long as there is no moral deliberation, the mystical psychology points to the same pattern of working.

In the illusionist teaching, imagination or discrimination is the creating agency of all kinds of evil, and hence of misery. As the Dharma is absolutely unaware of all distinctions, moral, psychological, and epistemological, which means the Unconscious, the seekers after it are to transcend discrimination in all its form and to see into the functioning of Prajñā itself. When this is done, *mushin* (*wu-hsin*) is realized, there is no 'mind' in all our doings, which is the so-called state of 'no-mind-ness'; this is a life of effortlessness, letting the Unconscious live its life.

The Unconscious cannot be held responsible for its deeds. They are above moral judgments, for there is no deliberation, no discrimination. The valuation of good and bad presupposes discrimination, and where this is absent, no such valuation is applicable. If it is at all applicable, it is for those who cherish discrimination, and as those living in the Dharma share the nature of the Dharma, or rather as they are of the Dharma itself, they are the Free Spirit, they live entirely for the love of God, they cannot be measured by the standards used for things finite, they are guiltless in every possible sense of the word.

In one of the Tun-huang Zen MSS. which are collected in my *Shao-shih I-shu*[1] we have the following dialogue: 'If the Tao (= the Dharma) universally prevails in all things, why is it criminal to destroy human life and not criminal to destroy a plant-life? The master answers: To talk about the criminality of a deed is an affair of human imagination, and concerns its effect in a world of events, and this is not at all the right way of viewing it. Just because a man has not attained the ultimate reason of the matter, he says he has committed a murder. So he has a 'mind' which bears karma, and he is said to be guilty of a crime. In the case of a plant-life, it has no imagination, and hence no ego-consciousness, and he who destroys it remains indifferent about it; he conjures up no ghost of imagination. The result is that no idea of criminality is involved here.

'He who is free from the idea of self views [the world of] form as if it were the grass of the field, and treats it as if cutting the grass. Mañjuśrī threatened Gautama with the sword, and Angulimāla applied his weapon upon the body of Śākyamuni. But they all belong to the group of beings whose minds are in perfect accord with the Tao, and one in the realization of the truth of no-birth. They all know that all things are empty like the creation of Māyā. Therefore, here is no reference to the idea of criminality. . . .

'It is like a fire in the field burning up all vegetation, like a gale blowing down all the trees before it, like the earth sliding down the hillside, like a flood drowning the animals; when your mind is attuned to this, all is swept before you. If, on the other hand, there is a "mind" in you which makes you hesitate and deliberate and feel uneasy, even the destruction of a mosquito will surely tie the knots of karma for you. . . .

'It is like the bee sucking the flower, like the sparrow

[1] *The Lost Works of Bodhi-Dharma.*

pecking at grains, like cattle feeding on beans, like the horse grazing in the field; when your mind is free from the idea of private possession, all goes well with you. But as soon as there arises in the mind the thought of "mine" and "thine", you are slaves to your karma. . . .'

According to this, when your mind functions with Nature, being no more harassed by the dualistic thoughts of good and bad, just and unjust, merit and demerit, Heaven and Hell, but inevitably as fire burns and water soaks, you are not responsible for whatever deeds you commit, and consequently no course of karma is attached to them. You behave like the wind, and who blames the wind when it leaves havoc in its wake? 'The wind bloweth where it listeth, and thou hearest the sound thereof, but canst not tell whence it cometh and wither it goeth' (*John* iii, 8). When you are like this, no karma can tie you up to any form of obligation or responsibility, though of course this does not mean that you escape the laws of causation which regulate this empirical world of ours. These laws may be artificial, human-made, being the outcome of moral deliberations, but they work just the same.

While your own mind is free from discriminative thoughts and feelings, other minds, not so free as yours, and given up to imaginations, will no doubt affect your life under the guise of moral laws. But these laws are like the wind too, or like the swinging of 'the sword that cuts the spring breeze in the flash of lightning'. We are reminded of Emerson's 'Brahma', and I quote the first stanza:

> If the red slayer think he slays,
>   Or if the slain think he is slain,
> They know not well the subtle ways
>   I keep, and pass, and turn again.

Emerson might have composed the poem in his study, quietly contemplating the Oriental trend of thought, and feeling something in his own mind which echoed the Orient; but the following is the verse uttered by a dying Japanese warrior under a shower of swords:

> Both the slayer
> And the slain
> Are like a dew-drop and a flash of lightning;
> They are thus to be regarded.

The last two lines are from the *Diamond Sūtra*, in which he was undoubtedly well versed.

In Shen-hui we have this: 'He who has definitely attained the experience of Mind retains his no-thought-ness (*wu-nien*) even when his body is cut to pieces in a mêlée between two fiercely contending armies. He is solid as a diamond, he is firm and immovable. Even when all the Buddhas, numbering as many as the sands of the Gangā, appear, not the least feeling of joy moves in him. Even when beings equal in number to the sands of the Gangā disappear all at once, not the least feeling of pity moves in him. He abides in the thought of emptiness and absolute sameness.'

This may sound terribly inhuman; but think of a great modern war in which hundreds of thousands of human lives are wantonly destroyed, and with this ruthless massacre before us we do not stop even for a moment, but plan another great war at its heels. God is apparently unconcerned with these trifling human affairs; God seems to have an infinitely grander idea of things than petty human imagination can paint. From Shen-hui's point of view a mustard seed hides worlds in itself as numerous as the Gangā sands, and quantities and magnitudes and anything based on intellectual discrimination mean to his unconscious nothing.

The *Diamond Sūtra* tells about a former life of the Buddha when his body was terribly mutilated by a despotic king:

'Subhūti, the Pāramitā of humility (patience), is told by the Tathāgata to be no-Pāramitā of humility, and therefore it is the Pāramitā of humility. Why? Subhūti, anciently, when my body was cut to pieces by the King of Kāliṇga, I had neither the idea of an ego, nor the idea of a person, nor the idea of a being, nor the idea of a soul. Why? When at that time my body was dismembered, limb by limb, joint after joint, if I had had the idea either of an ego, or of a person, or of a being, or a soul, the feeling of anger and ill-will would have been awakened in me. . . .'[1]

What is *mushin* (*wu-hsin* in Chinese)? What is meant by 'no-mind-ness' or 'no-thought-ness'? It is difficult to find an English equivalent except the Unconscious, though even this must be used in a definitely limited sense. It is not the Unconscious in its usual psychological sense, nor in the sense given it by the analytical psychologists, who find it very much deeper than mere lack of consciousness, but probably in the sense of the 'abysmal ground' of the mediaeval mystics, or in the sense of the Divine Will even before its utterance of the Word.

Mushin, or *munen*, is primarily derived from *muga, wu-wo, anūtman*, 'non-ego', 'selflessness' which is the principal conception of Buddhism, both Hīnayāna and Mahāyāna. With the Buddha this was no philosophical concept, it was his very experience, and whatever theory developed around it was a later intellectual framework to support the experience. When the intellectualization went further and deeper the doctrine of anātman assumed a more metaphysical aspect, and the doctrine of Śūnyatā developed. So far as the experience itself was concerned it was the same, but the doctrine of Śūnyatā has a more comprehensive field of application, and as a philosophy it goes deeper into the source of the experience. For the concept of Śūnyatā is now applied not only to the experience of egolessness, but to that of formlessness generally. The *Prajñāpāramitā Sūtras* all

[1] *Manual of Zen Buddhism*, D. T. Suzuki, p. 51.

emphatically deny the notion of a person, of a being, of a creator, of a substance, etc. Anātman and Śūnyatā are practically the same teaching. Along with Śūnyatā there comes Prajñā, which now becomes one of the principal topics of the Sūtras.

In Hui-neng's *T'an-ching* the Buddha-nature and self-nature are subjects of constant reference. They mean the same thing, and they are primarily by nature pure, empty, *Śūnyā*, non-dichotomic, and unconscious. This pure, unknown Unconscious moves, and Prajñā is awakened, and with the awakening of Prajñā there rises a world of dualities. But all these risings are not chronological, are not events in time, and all these concepts—Self-nature, Prajñā, and a world of dualities and multiplicities—are just so many points of reference in order to make our intellectual comprehension easier and clearer. Self-nature, therefore, has no corresponding reality in space and time. The latter rise from Self-nature.

Another point I have to make clearer in this connection is that Prajñā is the name given to Self-nature according to Hui-neng, or the Unconscious, as we call it, when it becomes conscious of itself, or rather to the act itself of becoming conscious. Prajñā therefore points in two directions to the Unconscious and to a world of consciousness which is now unfolded. The one is called the Prajñā of non-discrimination and the other the Prajñā of discrimination. When we are so deeply involved in the outgoing direction of consciousness and discrimination as to forget the other direction of Prajñā pointing to the Unconscious, we have what is technically known as *Prapañca*, imagination. Or we may state this conversely: when imagination asserts itself, Prajñā is hidden, and discrimination (*vikalpa*) has its own sway, and the pure, undefiled surface of the Unconscious or Self-nature is now dimmed. The advocates of *munen* or *mushin* want us to preserve Prajñā from going astray in the direction of discrimination, and to have our eyes looking steadily in the other direction. To attain *mushin* means to recover, objectively speaking, the Prajñā of non-discrimination. When this idea is developed in more detail we shall comprehend the significance of *mushin* in Zen thought.

To UNDERSTAND the scheme of thought conceived by Hui-neng and his school, the following interpretation may be of use to readers who are not used to the Oriental way of viewing the world.

What comes first in importance in the philosophy of Hui-neng is the idea of self-nature. But self-nature, I must warn the reader, is not to be conceived as something of substance. It is not the last residue left behind after all things relative and conditional have been extracted from the notion of an individual being. It is not the self, or the soul, or the spirit, as ordinarily regarded. It is not something belonging to any categories of the understanding. It does not belong to this world of relativities. Nor is it the highest reality which is generally ascribed to God or to Ātman or to Brahma. It cannot be described or defined in any possible way, but without it the world even as we see it and use it in our everyday life collapses. To say it is is to deny it. It is a strange thing, but as I go on my meaning will become clearer.

In the traditional terminology of Buddhism, self-nature is Buddha-nature, that which makes up Buddhahood; it is absolute Emptiness, *Śūnyatā*, it is absolute Suchness, *Tathatā*. May it be called Pure Being, the term used in Western philosophy? While it has nothing to do yet with a dualistic world of subject and object, I will for convenience' sake call it Mind, with the capital initial letter, and also the Unconscious. As Buddhist phraseology is saturated with psychological terms, and as religion is principally concerned with the philosophy of life, these terms, Mind and the Unconscious, are here used as synonymous with Self-nature, but the utmost care is to be taken not to confuse them with those of empirical psychology; for we have not yet come to this; we are speaking of a transcendental world where no such shadows are yet traceable.

In this Self-nature there is a movement, an awakening, and the Unconscious becomes conscious of itself. This is not the region where the question 'Why?' or 'How' can be asked. The awakening or movement or whatever it may be called is to be taken as a fact which goes beyond refutation. The bell rings, and I hear its vibrations as transmitted through the air. This is a plain fact of perception. In the same way, the rise of consciousness in the Unconscious is a matter of experience; no mystery is connected with it, but, logically stated, there is an apparent contradiction, which once started goes on contradicting itself eternally. Whatever this is, we have now a self-conscious Unconscious or a self-reflecting Mind. Thus transformed, Self-nature is known as Prajñā.

Prajñā, which is the awakening of consciousness in the Unconscious, functions in a twofold direction. The one is towards the Unconscious and the other towards the conscious. The Prajñā which is orientated to the Unconscious is Prajñā properly so called, while the Prajñā of consciousness is now called mind with the small initial letter. From this mind a dualistic world takes its rise: subject and object, the inner self and the external world, and so on. In the Mind, therefore, two aspects are also distinguishable: Prajñā-mind of non-discrimination and dualistic mind. The mind of the first aspect belongs to this world, but so long as it is linked with Prajñā it is in direct communication with the Unconscious, it is the Mind; whereas the mind of the second aspect is wholly of this world, and delighted with it, and mixes itself with all its multiplicities.

The mind of the second aspect is called by Hui-neng 'thought', *nen nien*. Here, mind is thought, and thought mind; *nien* (*nen*) is *hsin* (*shin*) and *hsin nien*. From the relative point of view, the mind of the first aspect may be designated 'no-mind' in contradistinction to the mind of the second aspect. As the latter belongs to this side of our ordinary experience, so called, the former is a transcendental one and in terms of Zen philosophy is 'that which is not the mind', or 'no-mind', or 'no-thought'.

To repeat, Prajñā is a double-edged sword, one side of which cuts the Unconscious and the other the conscious. The first is also called Mind, which corresponds to 'no-mind'. The 'no-mind' is the unconscious phase of the mind which is the conscious side of Prajñā. The diagram below will help to clear up this scheme of the Unconscious:

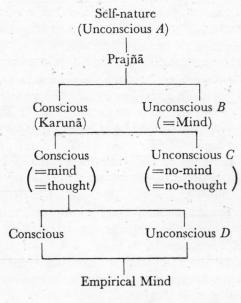

Self-nature
(Unconscious *A*)
|
Prajñā
|

Conscious (Karunā)   Unconscious *B* (=Mind)

Conscious (=mind =thought)   Unconscious *C* (=no-mind =no-thought)

Conscious   Unconscious *D*

Empirical Mind

DIAGRAM I.

In this the Unconscious *A*, *B*, and *C* belong to the transcendental order, and are essentially of one and the same nature, whereas the unconscious *D* is of the empirical mind which is the subject of psychology.

With the above interpretation of Hui-neng's Zen

thought, helped by the diagrammatic analysis, read the following definitions of *munen* (*wu-nien*), 'no-thought' or 'no-mind' gathered from the *T'an-ching*, and I hope Hui-neng will become more intelligible, and with him all the rest of the Zen masters cited above in various connections:

Hui-neng defines *wu-nien*, 'To have thoughts as not having them' (or would it better to translate: 'To have thoughts and yet not to have them'?). This evidently means to be conscious of the Unconscious or 'to find the Unconscious in consciousness', both of *C* grade above the empirical plane. A few lines below, Hui-neng has this for *wu-nien*: 'Facing all environing objects the mind remains unstained'; that is, no thoughts are raised in the mind. By 'environing objects' a world of consciousnesses is meant, and not to be stained in it pointed to the Unconscious, a state where no 'thoughts', no consciousness, interfere with the functioning of the mind. Here we recognize again the Unconscious of *C* grade.

The following statements by Hui-neng are quite clear without comments:

'Turning thoughts on Self[-nature], they are kept away from the environing objects; thoughts are not raised on the environing objects.'

'To raise thoughts towards the environing objects, and on these thoughts to cherish false views, this is the source of worries and imaginations.'

'What is *wu-nien*, no-thought-ness? Seeing all things and yet to keep your mind free from stain and attachment, this is no-thought-ness.'

'He who understands the idea of no-thought-ness has a perfect thoroughfare in the world of multiplicities. He who understands the idea of no-thought-ness sees the realm of all the Buddhas; he who understands the idea of no-thought-ness attains to the stage of Buddhahood.'

What Hui-neng wishes to express by the idea of *munen* (*wu-nien*, no-thought-ness) may be gathered from these quotations, aided by Diagram 1. But note, in regard to the diagram, that the Unconscious developing by degrees, as it were, down to the empirical mind has nothing to do with any form of grading. When it is analysed and shown in the form given above we are apt to imagine that there are grades in the Unconscious, in the sense that they are different in kind, and that in the lower ones there is nothing of the higher. This is not true, for all the Unconscious are merged in one another. When the one is thoroughly grasped all the rest will be comprehended. But at the same time we can say that the unconscious becomes purified, so to speak, as we rise from the Unconscious in the empirical mind, and that before we come to the unconscious Prajñā we have most thoroughly to purge all the conscious defilements belonging to the empirical Unconscious. This is, however, one practical point of view of Zen discipline; theoretically stated, all the Unconscious are of one taste.

As to what the awakening of Prajñā means in the system of Hui-neng, I have already repeatedly made references to it. But in order to avoid misunderstanding more quotations are here given:

'When one awakens genuine Prajñā and reflects its light [on Self-nature], all false thoughts disappear instantaneously. When Self-nature is recognized, this understanding at once leads one to the Buddha-stage.'

'When Prajñā with its light reflects [within], and penetratingly illumines inside and outside, you recognize your own Mind. When your own Mind is recognized, there is emancipation for you. When you have emancipation, this means that you are in the Samādhi of Prajñā, which is *munen* (no-thought-ness).'

'When used, it pervades everywhere, and yet shows no attachment anywhere. Only keep your original Mind pure and let the six senses run out of the six portals into the six dust[-worlds]. Free from stain, free from confusion, [the mind] in its coming and going is master of itself, in its functioning knows no pause. This is the Samādhi of Prajñā, a masterly emancipation, and known as the deed of no-thought-ness.'

The Samādhi of Prajñā so called is the Unconscious itself. When Prajñā is entirely directed towards Self-nature and its other direction is ignored, it extricates itself, if we can say so, from its own contradictory nature and is itself. This is a dialectical contradiction inherent in our experiences, and there is no escape from it; in fact all our experiences, which means our life itself, are possible because of this supreme contradiction. To escape it is the sign of a confused mind. Therefore, says Hui-neng:

'As to not making your mind move towards anything, this is extirpating thoughts, which means being bound up in the Dharma, and is known as a perverting view.'

This citation may not be quite clear, as it has a historical significance. At the time of Hui-neng, indeed prior to him and even after him, there were some who endeavoured to escape the fundamental contradiction inherent in life itself by destroying all thought-activities, so that there was a state of absolute void, of utter nothingness, of negation imagined to be most thoroughgoing. Such are killing life itself, deceiving themselves thereby to gain it in its true form. They bind themselves by false ideas, taking the Dharma for annihilation. In point of fact, however, annihilation in any form is impossible; what one imagines to be such is simply another way of affirmation. However violently or boisterously one may protest, no shrimps can get out of the closed-up basket.

Hui-neng's idea of *wu-nien*, which constitutes the central thought of Zen teaching, is continued naturally in the *Sayings of Shên-hui*, and then more definitely explained, as already set out. Let us now quote Te-shan and Huang-po. One of Te-chan's sermons reads thus:

'When you have nothing disquieting within yourself, do not try to seek anything outside. Even when you gain what you seek, this is not real gain. See to it that you have nothing disquieting in your mind, and be "unconscious" about your affairs.[1] Then there will be Emptiness which functions mysteriously, vacuity which works wonders. When you start to talk about the beginning and the end of this [mystery], you deceive yourself. Cherish an iota of thought, and this will cause karma to work, which puts you on evil paths. Allow a flash of imagination to cross your mind, and you will put yourself in bondage for ten-thousand *kalpas*. Such words as holiness and ignorance are no more than idle names; excellent forms and inferior shapes are both mere illusions. If you hanker after them, how can you escape complications? But trying to shun them will also bring great calamities upon you. In either case all ends in utter futility.'

Huang-po Hsi-yun, in the beginning of his book, to which reference has already been made, alludes to the Mind which is the Buddha, and outside which there is no way to realize Enlightenment. The Mind means 'no-mind-ness', to attain which is the ultimate end of the Buddhist life. Read the following in the light of Diagram 1, and also in connection with Hui-neng's idea of Buddhahood, and the central teaching of Zen will become more comprehensible.

'The Master (Huang-po Hsi-yun) said to P'ei-hsin: Both the Buddhas and all sentient beings are of one Mind only, and there are no other dharma (objects). This Mind has no beginning, was never born, and will never pass away; it is neither blue nor yellow; it has no shape, no form; it does not belong to [the category of] being and non-being; it is not to be reckoned as new or old; it is neither short nor long, neither large nor small; it transcends all measurements, nameability, marks of identification, and forms of antithesis. It is absolute thisness; the wavering of a thought at once misses it. It is like vacuity of space, it has no boundaries, it is altogether beyond calculation.

[1] See p. 132 *et seq.* for fuller explanation.

'There is just this One Mind, which constitutes Buddha-hood, and in it are the Buddhas and all sentient beings, showing no distinction, only that the latter are attached to form and seek [the Mind] outside themselves. Thus the more they seek, the farther it is lost. Let the Buddha seek himself outside himself, let the Mind seek itself outside itself, and to the end of time there will be no finding. Stop your thoughts, forget your hankerings, and the Buddha reveals himself right before your eyes.

'This Mind is no other than the Buddha, and the Buddha is no other than sentient beings. When it is sentient beings, this Mind shows no decrease; when it is the Buddha, it shows no increase. It inherently holds within itself all the six virtues of perfection, all the ten-thousand deeds of good-ness, and all the merits numbering as many as the Gangā sands; there is in it nothing added from outside. When conditions present themselves before it, it gives itself freely; but when conditions cease, it becomes quiet. Those who have no firm faith in this Mind, which is the Buddha, and seek merit by attaching themselves to form and going through various disciplinary measures, cherish false ideas which are not in accord with the Tao.

'This Mind is the Buddha, and there are no Buddhas besides this, nor are there any other minds [which are the Buddha]. The purity of the Mind is like the sky with not a speck of form in it. When a mind is raised, when a thought is stirred, you turn away from the Dharma itself, which is known as attaching to form. Since beginningless time there have never been Buddhas attached to form. If you wish to attain Buddhahood by practising the six virtues of per-fection and all the ten-thousand deeds of goodness, this is prescribing a course, and since beginningless time there have never been Buddhas graduating from a prescribed course. Only have an insight into One Mind, and you find that there is not a thing which you can claim to be your own. This constitutes true Buddhahood.

'The Buddha and sentient beings, they are of One Mind and there are no distinctions. It is like space with no mixtures, with nothing destructible in it; and it is like the great sun illumining the four worlds. When the sun rises, brightness fills the world, but space itself is not bright; when the sun sets, darkness fills the world, but space itself is not dark. Brightness and darkness are conditions, replacing each other; as for the characteristic vast vacuity of space, it remains ever unchanged. The Mind which constitutes the Buddha and all sentient beings is like that; if you regard the Buddha as a form which is pure, bright, and emancipated, and sentient beings as a form which is soiled, murky, benighted, and subject to birth and death, you cannot, as long as you hold this view, attain enlightenment even after the lapse of *kalpas* equal to the Gangā sands, because you are attached to form. You should know that there is One Mind only, and besides this there is not an atom of anything you can claim to be your own.

'The Mind is no other than the Buddha himself. Truthseekers of this day fail to understand what this Mind is, and, raising a mind on the Mind, seek the Buddha in a world outside it, and attaching themselves to form practise discipline. This is a bad way, and not at all the one leading to enlightenment.

'[It is said that] it is better to make offerings to one monk who has realized no-mind-ness (*wu-hsin*) than to make offerings to all the Buddhas of the ten quarters. Why? No-mind-ness means having no mind (or thoughts) whatever. The body of Suchness inwardly is like wood or stone; it is immovable, unshakable; outwardly, it is like space where one knows no obstructions, no stoppage. It transcends both subject and object, it recognizes no points of orientation, it has no form, it knows neither gain nor loss. Those who run [after things outside] do not venture to enter into this Dharma, for they imagine that they will fall into a state of nothingness where they are completely

131

at a loss what to do. Therefore they just give it a glance and beat a retreat. Thus they are generally seekers of wide learning. Indeed, those seekers of wide learning are like hairs [i.e. too many], whereas those who understand the truth are like horns [i.e. too few].'

Chinese expressions, especially those used in connection with Zen thought, are full of significance which, when translated into such languages as English, loses altogether its original suggestiveness. The very vagueness so characteristic of the Chinese style of writing is in fact its strength: mere points of reference are given, and as to how to connect them, to yield a meaning, the knowledge and feeling of the reader are the real determinant.

Zen, being no believer in verbosity, uses, when pressed for expression, the fewest possible words, not only in its regular, formal '*mondo*' (dialogue), but in all ordinary discourse in which Zen thought is explained. In Huang-po's sermon, quoted above, and also in Te-shan's, we come across some highly significant phrases, one of which by Te-shan is *tan wu shih yu hsin, wu hsin yu shih*, and another by Huang-po, *chih hsia wu hsin*. Here is the gist of Zen teaching. Te-shan's is literally 'only [have] nothing in the mind, have no-mind in things': while Huang-po's is 'Immediately-down [have] no-mind.'

Both in Te-shan and Huang-Po, Zen is taught to be something in direct contact with our daily life; there are no speculations soaring heavenward, no abstractions making one's head reel, and no sentimental sweetness which turns religion into a love-drama. Facts of daily experience are taken as they come to us, and from them a state of no-mind-ness is extracted. Says Huang-po in the above citations: 'The original Mind is to be recognized along with the working of the senses and thoughts; only it does not belong to them, nor is it independent of them.' The Unconscious, the recognition of which makes up *mushin*, lines every experience which we have through the senses and thoughts. When we have an experience, for example, of seeing a tree, all that takes place at the time is the perceiving of something. We do not know whether this perception belongs to us, nor do we recognize the object which is perceived to be outside ourselves. The cognition of an external object already presupposes the distinction of outside and inside, subject and object, the perceiving and the perceived. When this separation takes place, and is recognized as such, and clung to, the primary nature of the experience is forgotten, and from this an endless series of entanglements, intellectual and emotional, takes its rise.

The state of no-mind-ness refers to the time prior to the separation of mind and world, when there is yet no mind standing against an external world and receiving its impressions through the various sense-channels. Not only a mind, but a world, has not yet come into existence. This we can say is a state of perfect emptiness, but as long as we stay here there is no development, no experience; it is mere doing-nothing, it is death itself, so to speak. But we are not so constituted. There rises a thought in the midst of Emptiness; this is the awakening of Prajñā, the separation of unconsciousness and consciousness, or, logically stated, the rise of the fundamental dialectical antithesis. *Mushin* stands on the unconscious side of the awakened Prajñā, while its conscious side unfolds itself into the perceiving subject and the external world. This is what Huang-po means when he says that the original Mind is neither dependent upon nor independent of what is seen (*dṛiṣṭa*), heard (*śruta*), thought (*mata*) or known (*jñāta*). The Unconscious and the world of consciousness are in direction opposition, yet they lie back to back and condition each other. The one negates the other, but this negation is really affirmation.

Whatever this may be, Zen is always close to our daily experience, which is the meaning of Nansen's (Nan-ch'uan's) and Baso's (Ma-tsu's) utterance: 'Your everyday mind (thought) is the Tao.' 'When hungry, we eat, and when tired, we sleep.' In this directness of action, where there are no mediating agencies such as the recognition of objects, consideration of time, deliberation on values, etc., the Unconscious asserts itself by negating itself. In what follows,[1] I give the practical workings of the Unconscious as experienced by the masters who try hard to teach it to their pupils.

1. Hsiang-nien of Shou-shan (925–992) was asked: 'According to the Sūtra, all the Buddhas issue out of this Sūtra; what is this Sūtra?' 'Softly, softly!' said the master. 'How do I take care of it?' 'Be sure not to get it stained.' To make this *mondo* more intelligible to the reader, 'this Sūtra' does not necessarily mean the *Prajñāpāramitā* where the phrase occurs: it may be taken to mean Hui-neng's Self-nature, Huang-po's Original Mind, or in fact anything which is generally considered the Ultimate Reality from which all things take their rise. The monk now asks what is this Great Source of all things. As I said before, this conception of Great Source as existing separately somewhere is the fundamental mistake we all make in our attempt intellectually to interpret our experience. It is in the nature of the intellect to set up a series of antitheses in the maze of which it loses itself. The monk was no doubt a victim to this fatal contradiction, and it is quite likely that he asked the question 'What is this Sūtra?' at the top of his voice. Hence the master's warning: 'Softly, softly.' The text does not say whether this warning was readily taken in by the source of all the Buddha himself, but the next question as to how to take care of it (or him) shows that he got some insight into the matter. 'What?', 'Why?', 'Where?', and

---

[1] The examples are taken almost at random from the *Records of the Transmission of the Lamp* (*Chuan-ting Lu*). This is a mine of such records, chiefly of the T'ang, Five Dynasties, and early Sung periods, roughly A.D. 600–1000.

'How?'—all these are questions irrelevant to the fundamental understanding of life. But our minds are saturated
with them, and this fact is a curse on us all. Hsiang-nien
fully realized it, and does not attempt any intellectual
solution. His most practical matter-of-fact answer, 'Softly,
softly!', was enough to settle the gravest question at one
blow.

2. A monk asked Hsiang-nien: 'What is the Body of
space?' Space may here be translated as the sky or void;
it was conceived by ancient people to be a kind of objective
reality, and the monk asks now what supports this void,
what is its Body around which this vast emptiness hangs.
The real meaning of the question, however, does not
concern the vacuity of space, but the monk's own state
of mind, at which he arrived probably after a long meditation practised in the conventional manner; that is,
by wiping thoughts and feelings off his consciousness. He
naturally imagined, like so many Buddhists as well as lay-
people, that there was a being, though altogether inde-
finable, still somehow graspable as supporter of the un-
supported. The master's answer to this was: 'Your old
teacher is underneath your feet.' 'Why, Reverend Sir, are
you underneath the feet of your own pupil?' The master
decided: 'O this blind fellow!' The monk's question sounds
in a way abstruse enough, and if Hsiang-nien were a
philosopher he would have discoursed at great length.
Being, however, a practical Zen master who deals with
things of our daily experience, he simply refers to the spatial
relation between himself and his pupil, and when this is not
directly understood and a further question is asked, he is
disgusted, and despatches the questioner with a slighting
remark.

3. Another time Hsiang-nien was approached with this
request: 'I, a humble pupil of yours, have been troubled
for long with an unsolved problem. Will you be kind
enough to give it your consideration?' The master brus-

quely answered: 'I have no time for idle deliberation.' The monk was naturally not satisfied with this answer, for he did not know what to make of it. 'Why is it so with you, Reverend Sir?' 'When I want to walk, I walk; when I want to sit, I sit.' This was simple enough; he was perfect master of himself. He did not need any deliberation. Between his deed and his desire there was no moral or intellectual intermediary, no 'mind' interfered, and consequently he had no problems which harassed his peace of mind. His answer could not be anything but practical and truly to the point.

4. A monk asked Hsiang-nien: 'What is your eye that does not deceive others?' This is a liberal translation; the question really demands the expression of the master's genuine, undeceiving attitude of mind which controls all his experiences. Our eye is generally found covered with all kinds of dust, and the refraction of light thereby caused fails to give us the correct view of things. The master responded right away, saying: 'Look, look, winter is approaching.'

Probably this *mondo* took place in a mountain monastery surrounded with trees, now bare and trembling in the wind, and both were looking at the snow-bearing clouds. The approach of the winter was quite certain; there was no deception about it. But the monk wondered if there were not something more than that and said: 'What is the ultimate meaning of it?' The master was perfectly natural and his answer was: 'And then we have the gentle spring breeze.' In this there is no allusion to deep metaphysical concepts, but a plain fact of observation is told in the most ordinary language. The monk's question may elicit in the hands of the philosopher or theologian quite a different form of treatment, but the Zen master's eye is always on facts of experience accessible to everybody, and verifiable by him whenever he wants. Whatever mysticism enveloped the master was not on his side, but on the side of him who looks for it because of his own blindness.

These passages are enough to show the Zen masters' attitude towards the so-called metaphysical or theological questions which torment so many people's religiously susceptible hearts, and also the method they use in handling the questions for the edification of their pupils. They never resort to discussions of a highly abstract nature, but respect their daily experiences, which are ordinarily grouped under the 'seen, heard, thought, and known'. Their idea is that in our 'everyday thought' (*ping-chang hsin*) the Unconscious is to be comprehended, if at all; for there is no intermediary between it and what we term 'the seen, heard, thought, and known'. Every act of the latter is lined with the Unconscious. But to impress my readers to the point of tiresomeness, I will give a few more examples.

5. A monk asked Ta-tung of T'ou-tzu Shan: 'When the Prince Nāta returns all the bones of his body to his father, and all the flesh to his mother, what remains of his Original Body?'

Ta-tung threw down the staff which was in his hand.

The question is really a very serious one, when conceptually weighed, as it concerns the doctrine of *anātman* so called. When the five *skandhas* are broken up, where does the person go which was supposed to be behind the combination? To say that the five *skandhas* are by nature empty and their combination an illusion is not enough for those who have not actually experienced this fact. They want to see the problem solved according to the logic which they have learned since the awakening of consciousness. They forget that it is their own logic which entangles them in this intellectual *cul-de-sac*, from which they are at a loss how to get out. The teaching of *anātman* is the expression of an experience, and not at all a logical conclusion. However much they try to reach it by their logical subtleties they fail, or their reasoning lacks the force of a final conviction.

Since the Buddha, many are the masters of the Abhidharma who have exhausted their power of ratiocination to establish logically the theory of *anātman*, but how many Buddhists or outsiders are there who are really intellectually convinced of the theory? If they have a conviction about this teaching it comes from their experience and not from theorizing. With the Buddha, an actual personal conviction came first; then came a logical construction to back up the conviction. It did not matter very much indeed whether or not this construction was satisfactorily completed, for the conviction, that is the experience itself, was a *fait accompli*.

The position assumed by the Zen masters is this. They leave the logical side of the business to the philosopher, and are content with conclusions drawn from their own inner experiences. They will protest, if the logician attempts to deny the validity of their experience, on the ground that it is up to the logician to prove the fact by the instruments which he is allowed to use. If he fails to perform the work satisfactorily—that is, logically to confirm the experience—the failure is on the side of the logician, who has now to devise a more effective use of his tools. The great fault with us all is that we force logic on facts whereas it is facts themselves that create logic.

6. A monk asked Fu-ch'i: 'When the conditions (such as the four elements, five *skandhas*, etc.) are dispersed, they all return to Emptiness, but where does Emptiness itself return?' This is a question of the same nature as the one cited concerning the original body of Prince Nata. We always seek something beyond or behind our experience, and forget that this seeking is an endless regression either way, inward or outward, upward or downward. The Zen master is well aware of this, and avoids the complications. Fu-ch'i called out, 'O Brother!' and the monk answered: 'Yes, Master.' The master now asked: 'Where is Emptiness?' The poor monk was still after conceptual images, and completely failed to realize the whereabouts of Emptiness. 'Be pleased to tell me about it.' This was his second re-

quest. The master had no more to say, but quizzically added: 'It is like a Persian tasting red pepper.'

In his day—that is, in the T'ang period—the Chinese capital must have harboured people from the various strange countries of the West, and we find, as in the present case, references to Persians (*po-ssu*) in Zen literature. Even Bodhi-Dharma, the founder of Zen Buddhism in China, was regarded by some to be a Persian, perhaps by this no more than a man from a foreign country. Evidently some T'ang historians did not distinguish Persians from Indians. By a Persian tasting red pepper, the master means his inability to express the experience in the proper Chinese words, being a stranger to the country.

7. A monk came to T'ou-tzu and asked: 'I have come from a distant place with the special intention of seeing you. Will you kindly give me one word of instruction?' To this, the master replied: 'Growing old, my back aches today.' Is this one word of instruction in Zen? To a pilgrim who has come a long way from the remotest part of the country to be specially instructed by the old master, 'My back aches' seems to be giving the cold shoulder—altogether too cold. But it all depends how you look at the matter. Inasmuch as Zen deals with our everyday experience, this old master's expression of pain in his back must be regarded as directly pointing to the primary Unconscious itself. If the monk were one who had long pondered on the matter, he would at once see where T'ou-tzu is trying to make him look.

But here is a point on which to be on guard concerning the conception of the Unconscious. Although I have repeatedly given warnings on the subject, I here quote T'ou-tzu again. A monk asked him: 'How about not a thought yet arising?' This refers to a state of consciousness in which all thoughts have been wiped out and there prevails an emptiness; and here the monk wants to know if this points to the Zen experience; probably he thinks he has come to the realization itself. But the master's reply was: 'This is really nonsensical!' There was another monk who came to another master and asked the same question, and the master's answer was: 'Of what use can it be?' Evidently the master had no use for the state of unconsciousness conceived by most Buddhists.

T'ou-tzu on another occasion was asked: 'What about the time when the golden cock has not yet crowed?' This purports to cherish the same view as expressed by the two preceding monks. T'ou-tzu said: 'There is no sound.' 'What after the crowing?' 'Everybody knows the time.' Both are matter-of-fact answers, and we may wonder where this mysterious, elusive, incomprehensible Zen may be.

To imagine that Zen is mysterious is the first grave mistake which many make about it. Just because of this mistake the Unconscious fails to act in its unconscious way, and the real issue is lost in conceptual entanglements. The mind is divided between two opposing concepts, and the result is unnecessary worry. The following illustrates the way to avoid the contradiction, or rather to live it, for life is in reality a series of contradictions. A monk asked T'ou-tzu: 'Old Year is gone and New Year has arrived: is there one thing that has no relation whatever to either of the two, or not?'

As has already been seen, Zen is always practical, and lives with events of daily occurrence. The past is gone and the present is here, but this present will also soon be gone, indeed it is gone; time is a succession of these two contradicting ideas, and everything which takes place in this life of ours bestrides the past and present. It cannot be said to belong to either of the two, for it cannot be cut in pieces. How, then, does an event of the past go over to the present so that we have a complete conception of the event as complete? When thought is divided like this, we may come to no conclusion. It is thus for Zen to settle the matter in the most conclusive manner, which is in the most practical manner. Therefore, the master answered the monk's question: 'Yes.' When it was asked again 'What is it?' the master said: 'With the ushering of New Year, the entire world looks rejuvenated, and all things sing "Happy New Year".'

In order to explain how one comes to realize the state of *mushin* (*wu-hsin*) or *munen* (*wu-nien*), I have given a diagrammatic analysis of Self-nature, as the term is used in the *T'an-ching*. The diagram is what I may call the temporal view of Self-nature, and when it is not supplemented by the spatial explanation, the idea is liable to be misunderstood.

The awakening of Prajñā in the body of Self-nature, whereby the Conscious is differentiated from the Unconscious, may suggest that such an event took place in the remotest past, and that the present world, with all its multiplicities, confusions, and vexations, had sprung from it, and therefore that the object of religious discipline is to go beyond the present life and to reassert the original state of being. This is misleading and against the facts of experience. Buddhist philosophers often refer to 'the time which has no beginning', or to 'the very first' in which things were in a state of non-differentiation. This may suggest a process, and in combination with our diagrammatical analysis the conception of time may come to be regarded as essential. To avoid this misunderstanding, I append a 'spatial diagram' hoping to help the proper interpretation of the teachig of Hui-neng.

In fact, the concept of time is intimately connected with that of space, and no facts of experience yield their secrets unless they are surveyed at the same time from the spatial and the temporal points of view. The proper temporal view naturally implies the proper spatial view: the two are inseparable. The logic of Zen must be at once temporal and spatial. When we speak of the awakening of Prajñā, and of the differentiation of the Conscious and the Unconscious in the original unconscious body of Self-nature, we are in point of fact experiencing this awakening, this differentiation, this working of the original Unconscious in our daily, momentary passage of life itself. For life is not only lineal, succeeding in time, but circular, functioning in space.

The cylindrical figure (Diagram 2) represents the construction of our experience. Although it is cut into planes and confined within lines, in reality of course it has no such sections, nor is it confined in anything. Experience has no centre, no circumference, and the cylinder here merely serves to visualize it. Throughout the whole figure there runs a line of demarcation setting the Conscious against the Unconscious, but in Self-nature itself there is no such division, for it is the awakening of Prajñā in Self-nature which starts the whole machine functioning. Therefore, the Prajñā plane is bisected: Prajñā the conscious and Prajñā the Unconscious. Prajñā looks in two opposite directions, which is a grand contradiction, and from this contradiction there rises the entire panorama of our life. Why this contradiction? The contradiction comes from our asking for it.

Prajñā the Unconscious points to Self-nature, and is Self-nature. No-mind-ness is the issue of it and through Prajñā it is directly connected with Self-nature. Prajñā the conscious develops into the apperceiving mind where Self-nature comes in communication with the external world which acts upon the psychological mind, and is in turn acted upon by the latter. The apperceiving mind is where

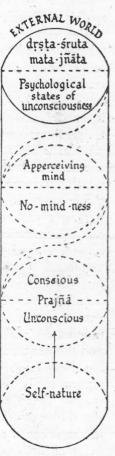

DIAGRAM 2.

we form the notion of selfhood, and when this notion forgets the fact that its very existence is backed by no-mindness, personal egoism is asserted. The Buddhist doctrine of Anatta is the same as the doctrine of no-mind-ness. That there is no ego-substance or ego-soul means that the notion of an ego is only possible by contradicting itself; that is, the apperceiving mind is no-mind-ness itself.

The unconscious mind has its pathological states on the plane of sense (*dṛiṣṭa-śruta*) and thought (*mata-jñāta*), corresponding to the 'Unconscious' of Analytical Psychology or Psycho-analysis. The Unconscious is the rendezvous of gods and demons. Unless one is properly guided by Prajñā and understands the meaning and function of the Unconscious, one is liable to fall into the black hands of the monster. The psycho-analytical Unconscious cannot go deep enough to include the question of no-mind-ness.

Diagram 3 attempts to explain the same fact of experience as the second, but from the spatial point of view. Below the bisecting line we have two divisions of the Unconscious, psychological and super-psychological. In the latter, Prajñā the Unconscious and no-mind-ness are included to show that they have for all purposes the same content. No-mind-ness gains its name in opposition to the empirical mind, but from the Prajñā side of experience it is no other than Prajñā itself.

Prajñā on the plane of the conscious may be said to correspond to the apperceiving mind. But the mind in its apperceiving character points to the plane of the *mata-jñāta*, whereas Prajñā is essentially of the Unconscious. If we follow some philosophers and postulate 'transcendental apperception', Prajñā may be said to share something of it. Ordinarily the apperceiving mind is occupied too much with the outgoing attention, and forgets that at its back there is an unfathomable abyss of Prajñā the Unconscious. When its attention is directed outwardly, it clings to the idea of an ego-substance. It is when it turns its attention within that it realizes the Unconscious.

This Unconscious is Prajñā on its unconscious plane, which, however, is too frequently wrongly recognized as the void, a state of utter blankness. Here is still a stain of

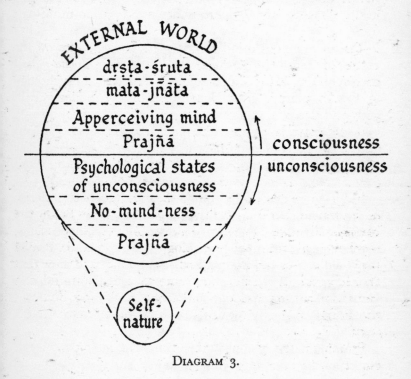

DIAGRAM 3.

dualism; the void so called still stands in opposition to being, hence the teaching of Anatta is disquieting to many people. They try to understand it on the plane of logic; that is, in antithesis to the notion of the ego. When, however, the teaching of Anatta is experienced, as when the Buddha uttered the following *gāthā*, it becomes free from logical complications, and there is no gaping abyss before

them, but a peaceful joy and a lasting sense of happiness.
The *gāthā* runs:

> Many a House of life
> Hath held me—seeking ever him who wrought
> These prisons of the senses, sorrow-fraught;
>   Sore was my ceaseless strife!
>
>   But now,
> Thou Builder of this Tabernacle—Thou!
> I know Thee! Never shalt Thou build again
>   These walls of pain,
> Nor raise the roof-tree of deceits, nor lay
>   Fresh rafters on the clay;
> Broken Thy house is, and the ridge-pole split!
>   Delusion fashioned it!
> Safe pass I thence—Deliverance to obtain.
>   *The Light of Asia.*

We are too apt to argue on the plane of the *Mata-jñāta*,
thinking of the apperceiving mind all the time. But experience purged of its intellectual fabrications never points
to the void but to rest and contentedness.

Those who fail to grasp the teaching of Anatta often
ask: Who is this contented one when there is no soul?
When this is logically answered to their satisfaction they
think that the teaching is absurd. But Anatta is not the
result of logical reasoning; it is a fact of experience. If
logic is needed here, take up the fact first and try to build a
logical structure about it, not conversely. If one form of
logic somehow fails, try another until satisfied. Let the
logicians remember this fact, that religion is experience and
in this sense irrational.

A monk asked a Zen master: 'What would you say when
both the mind and its objects are forgotten?' 'The mind and
its objects' means this world of relativity, where the subject
stands against the object, the knower against the known,

the one against the many, the soul against God, I against thee, and so on. To forget this means to transcend a world of dualities, and to be merged into the Absolute. Evidently the monk is following the course of logic as most of us do, as most Buddhists did in the day of the Buddha when, for instance, Maluṇkyaputta asked the Buddha about various metaphysical questions. The Buddha was always patient with his questioners, and, like the true Indian seer of the truth, quietly told them what constitutes the religious life apart from logically arguing about it.

But the Chinese Zen master is not so patient and grand-motherly, and when he does not beat his monks he gives out an utterly nonsensical reply. In the present case, Hung-t'ung of Yu-wang Shan, to whom the above question was put, gave this as an answer: 'A three-legged toad carries a huge elephant on its back.' What could such a dictum really mean? If it is not the climax of absurdity, it is at least highly disrespectful towards the earnest seeker of truth. Apart from its being disrespectful, however, the answer is meant to be absurd, irrational, and to make us go beyond the ken of logical understanding, so that we can discover a truth which directly expresses our experience itself un-coloured by intellection. Here lies the genuine kind-heartedness of the Zen master.

Before, however, this way of treating metaphysical problems found its way among the Zen masters of China, they were more 'rational', so to speak, and followed common sense. In one of the Tun-huang MSS. discovered recently, which contain an early history of Zen, we have the following story.

This was told by the Master Wu-chu of the T'ang dynasty for the benefit of his disciple called Wu-yu: 'I have a story. There was once a man standing on a high elevation. A company of several men who happened to be walking on the road noticed from the distance the man standing on a high place, and talked among themselves about this man. One of them said: 'He must have lost his favourite animal.' Another man said: 'No, it must be his friend whom he is looking for.' A third one said: 'He is just enjoying the cool air up there.' The three could not agree and the discussion went on until they reached the high place where the man was. One of the three asked: 'O friend, standing up there, have you not lost your pet animal?' 'No, sir, I have not lost any.' The second man asked: 'Have you not lost your friend?' 'No, sir, I have not lost my friend, either.' The third man asked: 'Are you not enjoying the fresh breeze up there?' 'No, sir, I am not.' 'What, then, are you standing up there for, if you say "no" to all our questions?' The man on high said: 'I just stand.'

In our daily life we are always arguing about things from the premise of an experience so deeply embedded in consciousness that we cannot get rid of it, and we are thereby enslaved. When we are awakened to this fact of slavery, we enter the religious life, and it is in this religious life that experience is all in all and there is no need for logic. To some minds, Buddhism appears ratiocinative, because of its reference to the Four Noble Truths, to the Twelvefold Chain of Orienation, to the Eightfold Path of Righteousness, etc. But we must remember that all these systematic arrangements are the after-product of the experience itself which the Buddha had under the Bodhi-tree.

In this respect Christianity and Buddhism are of the same order. Christianity may appeal more to the affective side of our life, while Buddhism appeals to its intellectual side, and for this reason Buddhism is regarded by some to be more scientific. But in truth Buddhism is based on personal experience as much as Christianity. This is especially the case with Zen Buddhism, which stands firmly on experience as the basic principle of its teaching. Therefore, all the doings and sayings in Zen point to this basis. There is no evading it, no going round it, no reasoning away of whatever absurdities may come up in giving expression to the fundamental experience. While a monk was attending on T'sao-shan, the master said:

'O Brother, it is terribly hot.'

'Yes, Master.'

'When it is so terribly hot, where should one go to escape the heat?'

'By throwing oneself into a boiling cauldron, into a scorching fire.'

'But when in the cauldron or in the fire, where should one go to escape the heat?'

'No pains reach here.'

Thereupon the master kept silent.

All this is the expression of life itself, and there is no intellectual arguing about it. If there were, the master and the disciple might have talked about otherworldliness, or about a land of bliss, or about some available summer resorts, or about egolessness. That they talked nothing of such, but stood firmly on the solid ground of our daily experience, most eloquently demonstrates the character of Zen. It is true that we cannot do without logic and philosophy because it is also the expression of life; to ignore it is nothing short of madness; but let us remember that there is another plane of life where only he is permitted to enter who has actually lived it.

A monk asked Hsing-chuan of Lo-shan: 'Why is not the stone gate of Lo-shan open to anybody?' The master said: 'O you stupid fellow!' 'If you unexpectedly come across a fellow of fine intelligence, would he be permitted to enter, or not?' The master answered: 'Have a cup of tea.' The entering into what some imagine to be the mystery of Zen is occasionally regarded as the most difficult thing in the world. But, according to this master, it is no more difficult than taking a cup of tea. At any rate, all arguing is on the plane of the *mata-jñāta*, as shown in Diagram 3. When one enters the plane of no-mindness it subsides, and Prajñā the

Unconscious controls the whole situation. To talk like this may already be deviating from the right Zen path. The point is to grasp the central key to the entire business.

A monk asked Fa-i of T'sao-an: 'It is said that when the mind is applied [to it] it deviates, when a thought is stirred it is contradicted; this being so, how does one proceed?' The quotation is from an ancient master, and means that the central mystery of Zen, if this expression is acceptable, is not to be comprehended by means of thought or intellection, and therefore that when the mind is applied and moves in that direction, the mystery will entirely elude one's efforts. If this is the case, the monk wants to know how he could ever make any advance in the study of Zen, for studying is a mental application, and the question is quite natural. The master answered: 'There is one whose mind is constantly applied that way, and yet there is no deviation in him.' 'How do things stand at this moment?' was the next question. 'There is a deviation already!' The awakening of Prajñā was the first grand deviation, and ever since we live in the midst of deviations. There is no way to escape them except living them as they follow one another. To say 'to escape' is already a deviation, a contradiction, a negation. 'Have a cup of tea!'; so runs Chao-chou's advice.

After surveying Hui-neng's Self-nature from the spatial as well as from the temporal point of view, what do we know of it? We have spent many pages in elucidating its Body, its Use and its Form, and have talked a great deal about it, but no more than that. 'About it' is not the same as 'it', and in matters religious understanding is experiencing, outside of which there is no way of getting at 'it'. No amount of abstractions avail any more than one word uttered on a most propitious occasion. A monk asked Chih-fu, of E-hu: 'What is the one word?' The master's counter-question was: 'Do you understand?' The monk said: 'If so, is that not it?'

The master sighed: 'Alas, no hope!' Another time a monk asked: 'What is your last word?'[1] The master said: 'What do you say?' The monk, who apparently thought the master failed to take his idea in, said again: 'What ought it to be?' 'Please don't disturb my nap,' was the master's cold reply.

[1] Literally, 'the first word'. But in cases like this it is the last word a Zen master would say about his Zen. It is 'the one word' which is in perfect accord with the experience.

151

ALL THESE Zen *mondo* may seem to outsiders simply nonsense, or purposely mystifying. But the most marvellous fact in the history of humanity is that this 'nonsensical' or 'mystifying' cult has been prospering for about one thousand five hundred years, and has engaged the attention of some of the best minds in the Far East. More than that, it is still exercising great spiritual influence in various ways in Japan. This fact alone makes Zen a worthy subject of study not only for Buddhist scholars but for all students of religion and general culture. This is, however, just to show to our readers that there is something in Zen pointing to the most fundamental fact of life which, when fully understood, gives one great religious satisfaction. All the *mondo* making up the annals of Zen are nothing but so many indicators giving expression to the experience gone through by the masters.

Let me conclude this Essay with the story of the monk Fu, of Tai-yuan, who lived in the beginning of the Five Dynasties (the eleventh century). He succeeded Hsueh-feng, and never undertook the task of presiding over a monastery, but contented himself with looking after the bathroom for his Brotherhood. Once when he was taking part in a religious service at Chin-shan, a monk asked him: 'Did you ever visit Wu-tai Shan?' Wu-tai Shan is noted as the earthly abode of Mañjuśrī. Pilgrims come here from all parts of the country, including Tibet and India, and it is said that to the sincere devotees the Bodhisattva manifests himself. The mountain is located in the province of Shan-hsi, in northwest China, whereas Chin-shan is in Southern China. Fu the monk answered: 'Yes, I once did.' The monk said: 'Did you then see Mañjuśrī?' 'Yes,' replied Fu. 'Where did you see him?' 'Right in front of the Buddha Hall at Chin-shan,' came promptly from his mouth.

When Fu came to Hsueh-feng, the latter asked him: 'I understand Lin-chi has three maxims,'[1] is that so? 'Yes, you are right.' 'What is the first maxim?' Fu the monk raised his eyes and looked up. Hsueh-feng said: 'That is a second maxim; what is the first?' Fu the monk folded his hands over his chest and went away.

When Hsuan-sha one day called on Hsueh-feng, the latter said: 'I have here among my Brotherhood an old hand, who is now working in the bathroom.' Hsuan-sha said: 'Well, let me see him and find out what kind of fellow he is.' So saying, Sha went out and found him in the act of drawing water for the bathroom. Said Sha: 'O Brother, let us have an interview.' 'The interview is all finished.' 'In what kalpa (age) did it take place?' 'O Brother, don't be dreaming'—which ended this strange interview.

Hsuan-sha came back to Hsueh-feng and said: 'Master, I have found him out.' 'How have you?' Sha then told him about the interview, and Feng concluded: 'You have been purloined!'

An, of Hu-shan, asked Fu: 'When your parents have not yet given you birth, where is your nose?' The nose has no special significance here; the question is tantamount to saying: 'Where are you prior to the existence of the world?' Zen likes to avoid abstract terms, highly generalized phrases, for they savour too much of intellectualization. To An's question Fu replied: 'Brother, you speak first.' An said: 'Born now! you tell me where he is.' Fu expressed his disagreement, whereupon An continued: 'Brother, what would you say?' Fu, without making any specific answer as we might expect of him, demanded to let him have the fan in the hand of Brother An. An handed it to him as requested, and repeated the first question. Fu remained silent and set the fan down. An did not know what to make of him, when Fu gave him a box on the ears.

When the monk Fu was once standing before the store-

[1] *Chu*=phrase, sentence, statement, dictum, etc.

house, a Brother monk approached and asked: 'It is said that wherever your eye may turn, there you have Bodhi.[1] What does this mean?' Fu kicked a dog which happened to be there, and the dog gave a cry and ran away. The monk made no response, whereupon Fu said: 'Poor dog, you were kicked in vain.'

From the relative point of view, in which we are all hopelessly involved, the questions of these monks seem to have sense enough, but as soon as they are taken up by the masters they invariably turn into gibberish or acts of madness, altogether beyond logic and commonsense. But when a man gets into the spirit, as it were, which moves the masters he sees that all this nonsense is the most precious expression of it. The point is not *'cogito, ergo sum'* but *'agito, ergo sum'*. Without realizing how, we are all the time deeply in the act of cogitation, and judge every experience of ours from the angle of cogitation. We do not go right into Life itself, but keep ourselves away from it. Our world is therefore always antithetical, subject versus object. The awakening of consciousness is all very well so far as it goes, but at present we have too much of it, failing to make good use of it.

The Zen masters desire us to look in the opposite direction. If we looked outwardly, they want us now to look inwardly; if we looked inwardly before, they tell us now to look outwardly. There is for them no diagrammatic analysis, temporal or spatial. They act 'straightforwardly', or 'whole-heartedly', to use one of the favourite phrases of the Zen masters. The highest act of our consciousness is indeed to penetrate through all the conceptual deposits and read the bedrock of Prajñā the Unconscious.

[1] This means that the Tao, or truth, is everywhere.

INDEX

ABHIDHARMA, The, 135
Abodeless (wu-chu), 102, 107
Abrupt Awakening, Doctrine of the, 20, 37, 55, 64
Abyss of Unknowability, The, 112
'All is mind-made' (Bodhi-Dharma), 115
An of Hu-shan, 153
Anarchistic naturalism in Zen teaching, 114
Anātman, the theory of, 137–8
Anatta, The Buddhist Doctrine of, 144, 146
Angulimāla, 117
Attainment of Buddhahood, 74, 129, 130
Avataṁsaka Sūtra, The, 90
Awakening of Faith in the Mahā-yāna (Aśvaghosha), 41
Awakening of Prajñā (The Unconscious becoming Conscious), 142–5. See also Diagrams 2 and 3, 143, 145

BEATING and rough treatment of Zen students by their Zen masters, 89, 90, 92, 94, 99, 101, 102, 108, 153
'Begone! You have no Buddha-nature', 94
Bodhi (The Tao), 54, 154
Bodhi-Dharma, Founder of Zen, 9, 25, 31, 102, 150
Bodhi-Dharma's sayings, 114, 115. See also Tun-huang documents.
Bodhisattva, The supreme knowledge of the, 16, 21, 50
Bodhisattva-Śila, The (cited), 33
Body, form and use: three concepts employed in Mahā-yāna philosophy to explain relation between substance and its function, 41, 42, 74 fn.

'Body of Space', The, 135
Brahma (poem by R. W. Emerson), 118, 119
Buddha, The, 83, 129, 131, 145, 147, 148. See also The Mind, 106
Buddhahood, The attainment of, 44, 54, 72–7, 126
Buddhahood, What constitutes, 106, 130
Buddha-nature, The; identical with the Self-nature or The Unconscious (see Diagram 1, 125), 121, 126, 129, 130, 131; primarily pure, 121; same in all beings, 51
Buddhism, early history of Zen, 15
Buddhism, Manual of Zen, 120
Buddhist Society, London, The, 6, 7

CATHOLIC DISCIPLINE, the, 68
Chang-hsing of Le-tan, 90
Chang-sha Ching, the kick of, 85
Chang-yen King, 29
Chao-chou's advice, 150
Chen-lang's question to Shih-tou, 97
Chi-chang of Kuei-sung Ssu, 92
Chi-ch'eng, the disciple, 18, 19, 20
Chien-hsing, to look into the nature of mind, 25
Chien-nin of Chen-chou, disciple of Ma-tsu, 87–8
Chih-fu of E-hu, 150
Chih-huang and Tai-yung: story of Zen masters, 34–5
Chih-hui, Chinese equivalent of Prajñā, 38
Chih of Yun-chu (8th century), teaching of, 78, 79
China, Zen thought in, 9, 85

155